Special Needs Assessment Handbook

for Specific Learning Difficulties

How to identify and address
barriers to learning

Charles Weedon

HODDER
EDUCATION
AN HACHETTE UK COMPANY

Acknowledgements

With thanks to colleagues, pupils and families at George Watson's College, Edinburgh, Perth Grammar School and Ballingry Junior High School, Fife, and to Serena Naismith, Head of Support for Learning, George Watson's College Junior School, Edinburgh, for her proof reading, advice and support.

Also available from Hodder Education:

Special Needs Assessment Profile Infant Check (SNAP-I)
Special Needs Assessment Profile – for social, emotional and behavioural difficulties (SNAP-B)
Special Needs Assessment Profile – for specific learning difficulties (SNAP-SpLD)
Special Needs Language and Literacy Assessment Handbook

Hachette UK's policy is to use papers that are natural, renewable and recyclable products and made from wood grown in sustainable forests. The logging and manufacturing processes are expected to conform to the environmental regulations of the country of origin.

Orders: please contact Bookpoint Ltd, 130 Milton Park, Abingdon, Oxon OX14 4SE. Telephone: (44) 01235 827827. Fax: (44) 01235 400454.
Lines are open 9.00–5.00, Monday to Saturday, with a 24-hour message answering service. Visit our website at www.hoddereducation.co.uk

First published in 2013 by Hodder Education, part of Hachette UK, Carmelite House, 50 Victoria Embankment, London, EC4Y 0DZ.

Impression number   5 4

Year   2017 2016

Typeset in ITC Stone Informal Std 11/14 points by Datapage (India) Pvt. Ltd.

Printed in Great Britain by Hobbs the Printers Ltd, Totton, Hampshire SO40 3WX

A catalogue record for this title is available from the British Library

ISBN: 978 1 444 19033 5

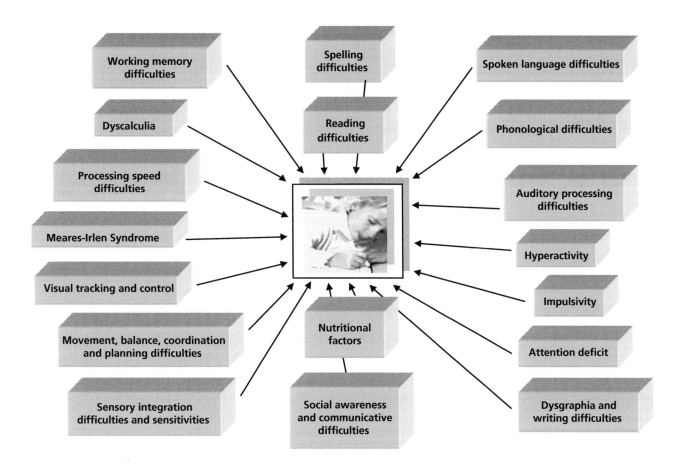

Many learners encounter *some* kind of **barrier to their learning**. These barriers are often made up of **several different strands of difficulty**. Focusing on the most obvious strands might often mean you miss some important ways you can make a real difference.

This simple and user-friendly book shows you how to **understand the wider picture** as well as how to **focus in on a learner's primary difficulty**, and **support effective learning**.

It is aimed at those involved in responding to children's learning difficulties – SENCOs and learning support staff. For the relatively inexperienced user, it should provide you with a comprehensive and useful starter kit. For the more experienced user, it should help both widen and deepen your understanding.

Charles Weedon

How to use this book

Using the whole book; or how to use this book in a hurry,
to find your way to the information you need today

PART 1

What are learning difficulties,
and how can they be identified?

This first part is about how you need to *think* about specific learning difficulties, and why it's usually not enough to depend on labels like 'dyslexia' and 'dyspraxia', or any of the others.

Part 1 is for *reading* more than dipping. You need to understand these core ideas so that you have an overview of what you are doing with the rest of the book. **Parts 2 and 3** are designed to be *dipped into as and when you need*, as you try to understand a pupil's learning and barriers.

PART 2

How to identify specific learning difficulties

This part is about identification and assessment – what to look for and how to identify each strand of difficulty.

PART 3

How to respond to specific learning difficulties

This part gives you ideas about what to do when you have identified each strand of difficulty – the practical follow-up.

So do at least skim Part 1, to orientate yourself, understand the landscape.... You can come back to it later to look at it more carefully when you feel the need.

But don't try to read through Parts 2 and 3 from start to finish. Just dip in to pick out the bits you need, when you need them.

Contents

PART 3   How to respond to specific learning difficulties

PART 1

What are specific learning difficulties, and how can they be identified?

Introduction: the nature of specific learning difficulties

Sometimes a child finds aspects of learning harder than you would have expected – reading, spelling, listening, sitting still, learning the tables, working with others.... Any or several of these difficulties may be evident, but you don't know *why*. You want to help – but without some clear idea about what the barriers might be, you are not too sure about just where to start.

This book sets out to help, and it is built around the idea that single-factor explanations of a child's difficulty are not enough. Looking for (and often finding) evidence of one or another kind of learning difficulty may be reassuring – but it may not answer all of your important questions.

For example, you may know that Jenny is an alert, articulate and well-motivated child, and that her poor reading and spelling seem to suggest some kind of specific learning difficulty. The word *dyslexia* jumps to mind. You know that she has some real strengths – but you know too that she is increasingly inattentive, and is beginning to talk about herself as being stupid. Her parents describe her as being increasingly reluctant to come to school.

Confirmation of a 'dyslexic' difficulty may be helpful. But it will be more helpful to go beyond this, to identify some of the precise strands that comprise Jenny's unique profile. If you had some evidence that her attention appears to be a significant problem, and perhaps the suggestion of a fatty acid deficit, as well as some evidence of dyspraxic difficulties and visual processing issues, then you might feel a little more confident about just where to start in setting out to help her. As well as help with reading and spelling, this is a child who might benefit from some nutritional supplements and some coordination/movement exercises, as well as referral to an optometrist to look at visual stress issues.

Effective assessment and intervention does need to be rigorous and *in-depth* – but it needs too to be *wide-angle*, so that you are not seduced by a single tidy label or category. You need more than that – so does the hypothetical Jenny. You need as well some insights into what makes *her* specific learning difficulty unique to her – only then can you feel more confident about where to start.

◆   ◆   ◆

You can use this book as you wish. You can read it through to gain an overview – and, as suggested, that's a good idea for Part 1, because that gives you a feel for each of the strands that might combine to create a barrier to a child's learning, and how they tend to cluster. Or you can dip in and select to find what you need at any one time – and that's probably the best way to approach Parts 2 and 3, which look at how to identify each of the strands, and how to respond to them.

In doing all this, the book makes use of familiar labels – *dyslexia, Asperger's and autistic spectrum disorders, dyspraxia, hyperactivity…* the list is a long one.

Labels and categories may indeed be helpful – they can *explain* all that accumulated failure and frustration and pain, and they can *empower*. But labels and categories have real limitations as well: to say, for example, that a child is 'dyslexic' is about as useful as saying someone has a fever. It describes what is being experienced – the outward behaviours and manifestations. But it tells you little about possible underlying causes, or about what you might be able to do to help.

The way in which any pupil with a difficulty learns is the endpoint of a developmental process that reflects the way in which he has drawn upon his own particular strengths to compensate for his own particular weaknesses – an ongoing dynamic that results in a way of learning that is likely to be unique to that learner. An underlying assumption in this book – one that makes it different and potentially more effective – is that there are, for example, as many 'dyslexias' as there are dyslexics, as many 'dyspraxias' as there are dyspraxics. That is, the barriers that are limiting the attainment of any single learner are unique to that learner, a unique combination of contributory strands.

The next section – *Exactly what are 'barriers to learning'?* – describes each of these strands in more detail. It looks at how, for most pupils with some barrier to their learning, there is something of a tangle of contributory strands, and suggests that looking for a single-category explanation of a child's difficulties will provide, at best, only part of an answer. To find evidence that justifies an 'ADHD' label – or a 'dyspraxia' label, or 'dyslexia' – may be helpful; but the evidence dancing tantalisingly in your peripheral vision may be just as important in suggesting how to help. Good assessment and identification must be 'in-depth' – but equally, it must be 'wide-angle'.

We look then at how some of these strands might typically *cluster together*. Knowing how they tend to cluster can make it easier when you decide which ones you need to look at in more detail for any particular pupil.

Part 2 looks at assessment and identification. It suggests how to gain this 'wide-angle' overview, as well as how then to probe for each strand of difficulty in more depth. The tests described in the text are simply those familiar to the author, and they include some 'composite' tests, or test batteries, that explore a range of characteristics of SpLDs. For the in-depth probing, some of the photocopiable resources from the **Special Needs Assessment Profile (SNAP-SpLD)** are provided, in Appendix 3.

Part 3 is about *responding* to each of the identified strands of difficulty. For most of the strands, particularly perhaps frequently-occurring ones like Reading and Spelling, the assessments and responses suggested will necessarily be samples selected from a far wider range of options. We all have our own preferred methods and strategies, and there is *no* attempt here to offer a comprehensive review.

The aim of this book is not therefore to suggest exactly how you should approach any given strand. Instead, it is to outline the wide range of strands you should be considering; and then, if you want to draw upon it, to offer *some* tried and tested ways of engaging with each strand. Again, the approaches described are those familiar to the author. Trust your own tried and tested techniques if you know they work.

For the sake of brevity, except where specific examples are given, teachers are referred to as female and pupils as male.

Exactly what *are* barriers to learning?

What *is* a **'specific learning difficulty'**, these **strands of difficulty** that combine to comprise a **barrier to learning**? In this book, it simply means some factor (or, more often, *cluster* of factors) that causes a learner to *under-perform* – to learn less effectively than he would if that barrier or difficulty were not there.

The idea of under-performing implies that people have a capacity or potential for academic success that can be impaired if some barrier is standing in the way. It implies that some learning difficulties tend to be more specific in nature, while others may be more general or global. This book is about the *specific* difficulties – it is about how to recognise and address these specific barriers.

For the young learner who has some such specific barrier, school can be a tough place. He's probably been a happy, active and curious toddler. Suddenly, he is expected to spend most of the day working at some of the things he finds hardest – sitting still, paying attention, learning early literacy skills. The bright and happy pre-schooler may become the uncertain and self-doubting school pupil. He probably learns quite early to keep his head below the parapet, attract as little attention as possible, and plug away at getting through the day with as little risk as possible. Unless he is socially confident and extrovert, his in-class behaviour will soon start to mimic those of a learner who has more general, global difficulties – and once that trajectory is set in place, it is hard to change. It feeds upon itself. Parents will have noted this change as their child moves from pre-school into formal schooling, probably with gathering concern and anxiety – but his teacher, who obviously did not know him before he started school, may gain quite the wrong impression of him as a learner, and respond to him accordingly.

The idea of **comorbidity** of learning difficulties is being accepted more and more – that is, a child with one obvious strand of difficulty is likely to have at least *some* other strands, some of which may be quite significant. Sometimes, these are simply 'adjacent' difficulties – for instance, a child might have poor spelling and handwriting as well as some intrinsic and separate difficulties with attention and impulsivity. Sometimes, one difficulty may be *causing* the other to some extent – the child with intrinsic difficulty in sustaining attention and staying on-task might not have focused too well on some of the less-than-gripping aspects of spelling acquisition, so that the attentional difficulty may be *causing* the literacy difficulty. Or it may run in the other direction: an intrinsic difficulty with acquiring automatic spelling will soon make spelling tasks seriously unrewarding and frustrating, so that attention becomes hard to sustain…. The literacy difficulty is *causing* the attentional difficulty. Either way, one weakness may quickly start to feed on another, establishing a down-spiral that can be hard to break.

The picture is certainly not all black – there are myriad examples of those who feel their learning **'difficulty'** should be seen instead as a learning

difference: acclaimed engineers, entrepreneurs, architects, surgeons, artists, and many others, sometimes speak of thinking and learning *differently* – and in such a way that, however tough school was along the way, they were enhanced rather than diminished by their unique way of learning. This needs to be remembered as the strands are looked at more closely: these barriers do make classrooms and exam halls hard places to be – but they can be managed and transcended, sometimes triumphantly so.

Remember, too, that you will certainly recognise *yourself* in some of the difficulties and barriers described below – many of these traits are there in many of us. It's only when one (or more) of them is prominent enough to stop you being able learn effectively, or to demonstrate your true level of competence, that it becomes a barrier to your learning. Don't be tempted to dismiss it, saying to yourself *'I'm a bit like that, and I've managed ok...'*. That may well be the case – and yes, you may also occasionally identify some apparently significant SpLD traits in a child who is nonetheless learning effectively.

That's the key question: *Is he learning as effectively as I think he should be learning?* If there appear to be some SpLD traits but he's doing well enough just now, then fine – no immediate action required. But it may still be an important 'heads-up'. He may be one of the many who is coping now, but whose coping strategies become increasingly inadequate as the threshold of demand rises – the one, say, whose teacher puzzles over in the exam years: *'Jamie's a bright lad – picks up new ideas quickly and effectively – but never manages to get anything like the grades he should in exams....'*

When that happens, then *do* take notice, *do* take action. The formal examination, time-constrained and hand-written, is our all-pervasive way – and for many learners *invalid* way – of measuring understanding and attainment. Arguably up to a quarter of the candidates in an exam hall may be disadvantaged to some extent, by some subtle barrier, or combination of barriers. **Don't be put off by the sceptics – there are plenty in every staffroom, as well the media.** Do whatever is needed, whenever it becomes apparent that maybe it *is* needed (see Part 3).

Taking these strands one by one, we start with Processing Speed Difficulties, because it's the one that crops up so very often, the common factor in so many of the clusters...

Processing speed difficulties are perhaps the commonest strand – by no means a universal feature of specific difficulties, but certainly pervasive. This is the youngster who *can* do the thinking, who *can* complete the task – but who seems to take an unusual length of time to do so. It may stem from slow processing of **visual** information; or it may be slow processing of **oral/aural** information; or it may be **both**. In reading, writing or copying, it may be a perceptual difficulty with the abstract visual symbols that comprise the alphabet – holding them in mind while working with them may take up a disproportionate amount of attention. It may be difficulty in forming them fluently. Or it may be in processing the *sounds* that the symbols represent – that feeling we all have sometimes of not being able to access and retrieve the word we want, so that our speech sounds a little laboured and effortful, an ongoing tip-of-the-tongue experience. Processing speed difficulties may sometimes be stand-alone – but more often they sit alongside other difficulties.

Working memory issues are equally pervasive. We all recognise these in ourselves – that failure to keep something at hand and accessible in memory while working with it. It can be frustrating and embarrassing: when you are being given information too fast, and you forget it even as you are listening to it; or you can't remember phone numbers long enough even to write them down, but have to ask for a repeat; or halfway through saying something, you forget exactly how it links into what you set out to say. It is as if your 'cognitive workbench' is too small, too cluttered – important items drop off it, nothing is at hand where you thought it was…. The implications for daily schoolwork are evident – learners are subjected to a continuous stream of information, and once it starts to jam or bottleneck, it backs up very quickly, and becomes swiftly unmanageable.

Spelling difficulties are often the most stubborn features of specific learning difficulties. They may be stand-alone, and be dignified with the splendid title of 'dysorthographia' (surely a 'must-have' category for the label enthusiast!). But far more often there will be weak handwriting and page layout as well – and where reading is good, so that the most obviously prominent barriers are with spelling and handwriting, **dysgraphia** is the most apt description.

Reading difficulties are seldom stand-alone strands – much more often they form part of the package of strands that typically comprise what is usually referred to as a **dyslexic** difficulty. These often present hierarchically, with spelling as the greatest weakness, then oral reading, but often with silent reading comprehension relatively better developed: when reading silently we can sometimes gloss over the kinds of barriers that impair our oral reading, so that intelligent use of context lets us grasp the ideas effectively enough.

This applies too to **Dyscalculia**. Certainly, there may be learners whose *sole* difficulty is a lack of any real sense of number, and with accessing number bonds or learning their tables – but much more often it is just part of the 'spaghetti syndrome' of strands that characterise specific difficulties. Certainly it is frequently found alongside the kinds of reading, writing and spelling issues that characterise dyslexic-type difficulties.

At a different level, **nutritional issues** may be contributing to any or all of the strands that comprise a learner's barriers. It is different in that it is primarily an environmental factor – but it is intrinsic in that physiologically we all have our unique tolerances and intolerances to what we eat and drink. For any significant barriers to learning, a child's whole diet should be considered – but in this context, the focus is on **Deficiencies of Essential Fatty Acids** as an aspect of nutrition that can affect some learning quite significantly, while also being easily addressed.

Phonological difficulties – a problem with processing and manipulating the underlying sounds that comprise the spoken word – are often part of literacy difficulties. Clearly, if you're not completely fluent and automatic in processing these underlying sounds, then you're going to find it relatively hard to encode the sounds into letters (writing in our alphabetic system) and to decode letters into sounds (reading at the decoding level). Phonological issues have often been seen as the core deficit underpinning dyslexic difficulties, but most people now accept that this cannot offer a full explanation.

Auditory processing difficulties may often be closely linked to phonological difficulties, though not always. These do not refer to any lack of auditory acuity as such – rather, they are inefficiencies in the ways in which auditory information is *processed* once it has been received.

Expressive and receptive language disorders have obvious implications for learning. Most of the skills and ideas we want to develop in children are conveyed through words – initially mostly spoken, but increasingly through the written word. If you find it hard in any way to receive, absorb, organise and develop ideas conveyed through words, then there exists a pretty big barrier between you and the world in which you must function and learn. Equally, if you cannot easily articulate and express your own ideas in a logical, organised, clear and coherent way, then the whole process of sharing your thoughts as part of developing them may be impaired. The implications for your learning are obvious.

In the same way that sound-based barriers can make it hard to learn to read and write fluently and effortlessly, so too can barriers that stand in the way of **visual processing**. Often lumped together as **visual stress**, they tend to derive from either **Meares–Irlen Syndrome** or **visual tracking and ocular control** issues – or, quite often, from elements of both.

Meares–Irlen Syndrome (formerly sometimes referred to as **Scotopic Sensitivity Syndrome**) is to do with a retinal sensitivity to the pattern of black parallel lines on a white background. Many of us experience this to some extent – try staring for a long time at any strong pattern of parallel lines, and you may well find that they start to shift and quiver a bit. For some, the parallel black lines on a white background that comprise text is enough to cause visual discomfort: sore eyes, wavering or indistinct lettering, tunnel vision, even nausea and migraines – any or all of these may be experienced to a greater or lesser degree.

Visual tracking and ocular control issues can cause equal difficulty. Fluent reading needs fluent eye movements and muscular control of the eyes. Where this is lacking, eye tracking can be slow and inefficient ('dysmetria' for the label-lovers...); or weak binocular convergence can cause eyestrain, making reading both slow and sore.

Dysgraphia is another strand that may be free-standing – the child whose only problem is appalling handwriting, page layout and graphic skills. But more often it is accompanied by dyslexic or dyspraxic (see below) strands of one kind or another.

Movement, balance, coordination and planning (dyspraxic-type) difficulties can affect almost everything we do. As well as making us physically clumsy or inept in one way or another, they can affect our ability to make and sustain friendships, our confidence and the ability to join in shared activities, as well making it harder to acquire a whole range of cognitive skills. For most of us, skills become automatic after a bit of practice – they need an enormous amount of attention at the beginning, but after a while you do them without thinking, without conscious attention. Remember learning to do hill-starts during driving lessons? It can be the same with skills like recognising and forming letters, sounding them out, learning number facts, and much else. For these children, there needs to be so much *more* practice if something is to become automatic. And even with a lot of over-learning, probably they still need to give it a disproportionate amount of attention. Multi-tasking remains a real challenge. We all know the child who can read aloud well enough, and whose silent reading comprehension is fine, but who can't do both these things at once without enormous effort. Often, too, these are the children who find it disproportionately hard to plan ahead, both in their personal organisation (often impressively chaotic!) and in planning and organising their ideas for written work.

Usually fairly obvious are any intrinsic difficulties in sustaining **attention**. The widely-used and perhaps over-used **ADHD** label (Attention Deficit Hyperactivity Disorder) is probably more usefully considered in terms of its typically constituent strands. **Attention Deficit Disorder** (ADD) is exactly what it suggests – it is the barrier facing the child whose attention wanders away again and again, however hard he tries to stay on task. It is right to be reasonably sceptical: it would be absurd to imply that loss of attention in class is necessarily a clinical condition of some kind. Boredom, hunger, mischief, laziness, sleepiness, the drone of the teacher's voice on a stuffy afternoon, or the intrinsic dullness of the task in hand (not all learning can be made exciting) – all these may and will cause loss of attention. But for some children the causes of inattention *are* genuinely intrinsic and neuro-physiological in nature.

It is much the same for the **hyperactive** child – the one in a constant state of fidget, of restlessness. In and out of his seat, head turning as if on a pivot to attend to every distraction (but seldom to attend to you), fingers tapping, knees in constant motion, hands forever seeking something to fiddle with.... As for ADD, there may be environmental explanations, and nutrition may well be a factor – but when these sorts of behaviour are persistent and significant, you're probably looking at a child who has some real neuro-physiological barriers to contend with. This child is probably among the most infuriating you've had to teach (and triply so if there are any Asperger's characteristics included in his particular mix) – but all these behaviours that make him so hard to have in the classroom are largely beyond his conscious control.

For many learning difficulties, it's probably true that the more a child perplexes, frustrates and baffles you, the more he needs your help. For this lad, it's truer than ever.

Impulsivity, often the third constituent strand of ADHD, may be stand-alone – the otherwise competent learner who responds without being ready to do so, who consistently blurts out his answers and ideas before he should, and who acts before thinking things through. But more often the impulsive learner is likely to be having to deal also with at least some hyperactive tendencies.

Sensory integration difficulties and sensitivities often occur alongside coordination difficulties, and/or behaviours that are associated with the autistic spectrum. These may be the children who object vigorously to certain foods or smells, who hate having their hair brushed or nails clipped, or can't cope with heights, or the roundabout at the play-park, or with rough and tumble play, or being jostled. At the cognitive level, the same integration and sensory difficulties may be affecting how they combine the sounds and shapes of letters or words.

These sorts of sensory integration and sensitivity issues are quite often seen in children with **social awareness and communicative disorders.** These are the children who sometimes seem to live in a world of their own – they may have a lot to say and often be very knowledgeable, but they talk *at* you rather than *with* you; they may want friends, but have no idea about the give-and-take of normal relationships. They seem not to be able to 'get inside the heads' of others, to empathise and see things through any eyes other than their own. They tend to take everything literally, and they find jokes and irony incomprehensible. They tend to like to have things just so, predictable and organised in the way they are used to and familiar with. Unexpected change can cause emotional meltdown. These behaviours are characteristic of many behaviours on the **autistic spectrum**, and of **Asperger's Syndrome**.

As so often, you may well recognise some of these traits in yourself, or in colleagues. 'Eccentric professor syndrome' often seems a more appropriate label – but often too there are difficulties for these children that can be eased a lot once they are recognised and understood.

These strands tend to be found in various different combinations, and one aim of this book is to make sure you don't miss any important ones when you're trying to understand and help a learner in difficulty.

But, importantly, the clusters discussed in the next section tend to align with the **categories of SEN** that often need onward referral by the school if the necessary extra help and support is to be provided.

The record sheets and examples in Appendix 1 and 2 show how you can use the outcomes to decide if one or more of these **SEN categories** might apply. The categories are:

◆ SpLD Dyslexia
◆ SpLD Dysgraphia
◆ SpLD Dyscalculia
◆ Dyspraxia/DCD
◆ Specific Language Disorders
◆ ADHD
◆ Autistic Spectrum Disorders (ASD)/Asperger's

As you'll see when you use the record sheets in Appendix 1, Sheet 1 records the strands of difficulty you have identified for a learner. Sheet 2 summarises the outcomes, and asks you to rate each strand of difficulty as **mild/ moderate/significant** for this learner, and it shows how the most relevant strands link to the **SEN categories.**

◆ Where you've described a strand as **Mild** or **Moderate**, these are **learning needs** that may be met within the school, perhaps with some further specialist support – as we did for 'School Action' and 'School Action Plus'.

◆ Where you've described a strand as **Significant** and it links directly to an **SEN category**, then you might want to **refer onward to an outside agency**. This is a learner who may need the support offered by a **formal SEN identification**, and in some cases an **Education, Health and Care Plan**.

Typical clusters of strands of difficulties

If specific learning difficulties are seldom 'stand-alone', are there *typical clusters* of strands? Are there characteristic profiles that might give you a 'heads-up', so that you can say 'Well, if I'm seeing *this* and *this*, then maybe I should be looking for *this* too ...'?

Yes and no.... Yes, there are typical clusters, and it's really helpful to be aware of them.... And No, they're absolutely not prescriptive. They can *guide* your thinking, alert you to important clues; but they mustn't *take over* your thinking. The key to understanding any child's learning difficulties is the recognition that the mix of strands for each child is unique. Think recipes: many excellent recipes have a common base – the onion, red pepper, tomato, dribble of wine.... But what makes one dish completely distinctive from another might be one or two small but key ingredients. Small differences in make-up, but *significant* differences in overall outcome – with specific barriers to learning, as with recipes.

Some examples may be helpful. Take five pupils who might be causing you and their families and teachers some concern – ranging from mild bafflement to nervous breakdown....

John S   has mainly **auditory processing problems**, causing **literacy difficulties** – let's call him the classic **'phonological dyslexic'.** Many of the research studies about dyslexia are based on the idea that dyslexia is a largely phonological problem.

Jenny J   has mainly **visual processing problems**, causing **literacy difficulties.** Some time ago, she might have been described as a **'visual dyslexic'**, before that idea became perhaps less fashionable.

Suzi M   has **dyspraxic and coordination issues, affecting literacy** as well as affecting how easily she makes and keeps friends. She is likely to be described as either dyslexic or dyspraxic – she's the dyslexic child who's also so very clumsy and disorganised.

Eric S   has **attentional and hyperactive difficulties** – they affect his learning as well as his behaviour, and he may well be the boy who seems to have all these **literacy difficulties**, but whose restlessness, defiance and behavioural difficulties sometimes seem more significant than the literacy difficulties.

Ahmed R has **autistic spectrum/Asperger's difficulties**, often **affecting literacy** to some extent, as well as the ability to **cope with school** and the **world around him.** He's the unhappy loner with obvious difficulties with learning – but often his behaviour and social/emotional/communicative difficulties seem to overshadow his other difficulties. His behaviour seems so strange, or rude, abrupt and egotistical that it captures his teachers' attention to the exclusion of much else.

These *aren't* separate and watertight categories – far from it. They often overlap, sometimes with dramatic effect – when Eric and Ahmed overlap, for example, so you have a child who combines ADHD and Asperger's, everyone is going to be desperate for support and advice! But still they're useful examples of why looking for a *single-category* answer often doesn't help.

Many of these children may present in class in a fairly similar way: poor literacy; lack of attention; attention seeking (or perhaps withdrawn); eccentric manner; poor handwriting…. On the surface, they may seem similar in certain ways – but the reasons for their difficulties may be very varied indeed.

For each of them, what might be the key features you should be alert for?

John S, the classic **'phonological dyslexic'**, is a quiet and hardworking boy, who finds reading and spelling really hard. He compensates as best he can by taking great care over his work – always beautifully presented, pencil always sharp, pencil case full of coloured pens. He gets on well with one other quiet boy in the class, but otherwise keeps himself to himself as much as possible.

Because he takes so few risks, and seldom offers ideas without prompting, it would be easy to see him as a nice lad, but just non-academic. But occasionally he says things that suggest a keen intelligence – a level of understanding that is somehow *never* reflected in his agonisingly short and painful pieces of written work.

As well as literacy difficulties, what might be the three key clues as to the precise nature of his learning difficulty? Probably they will be revealed through his difficulties with

♦ **processing speed**
♦ **auditory working memory – he just can't hold spoken information in mind for long**
♦ **some still apparent spoken language hesitancies and difficulties**

The ways in which he processes sounds and the spoken word are at the heart of his learning difficulties. Once you know this, you have a much better idea of how to help: focusing upon speech sounds, phonology and decoding skills are likely to be the most promising way forward for John.

Jenny J is the **'visual dyslexic'**, and she too is a focused and attentive pupil. She tries so hard, and gets so discouraged: reading, writing and spelling are so hard for her. She is increasingly aware that her friends seem to find these things so much easier than she does; and she's becoming increasingly unwilling to come to school each day.

As well as literacy difficulties, what might be the three key clues as to the precise nature of her learning difficulty? Probably they will be revealed through the way

- **she reads and copies so slowly**
- **her finger follows the line even when she's become an adequate reader**
- **she has headaches and sore eyes**

This is a girl who needs to see an optometrist or orthoptist, and who is likely to benefit from tinted specs or eye exercises, as well as help with her literacy difficulties.

Suzi M is the girl with the **dyspraxic and coordination issues, affecting literacy**. On the face of it, she presents as the most typical 'dyslexic' – she takes forever over a piece of work, and it looks a mess however hard she tries. Reading and spelling are not that good, but it is her chaotic lack of organisation that drives her parents and her teachers to distraction.

As well as literacy difficulties, what might be the three key clues as to the precise nature of her learning difficulty? Probably she is the girl with

- **a noticeably clumsy pencil grip**
- **chaotic personal organisation and self-management**
- **a real dislike of PE and ball games**

But addressing just her literacy difficulties would mean you're continuing to build on the shakiest of foundations – it might be really helpful for her to try to improve her underlying coordination, movement and coordination skills.

Eric S has **attentional and hyperactive difficulties** – they affect his learning as well as his behaviour. This lad behaves as if he's wired to the mains, permanently fidgeting and shifting about, and his attention is all over the place. He's the one whose occasional absence causes a guilty sigh of relief – it's so much easier to get on with the day's teaching when he's not there.

Probably he will indeed have poorly developed literacy skills, and it may be tempting to decide to address these first, in the hope that improved core skills will let him engage more effectively with the curriculum, and that his restlessness, defiance and behavioural difficulties will diminish as a result.

As well as literacy difficulties, what might be the three key clues as to the precise nature of his difficulty? He is likely to be the boy who

- **never thinks before he acts**
- **is forever on the move, and intrudes on others, and really doesn't seem able to manage his own behaviour**
- **can't sustain his attention to anything that doesn't intrinsically interest him**

It's very plausible that the inattention and hyperactivity *cause* the learning difficulties, rather than vice-versa. So helping him manage his attention and activity needs to come *before* you set about helping him develop his literacy skills.

Ahmed's **autistic spectrum/Asperger's** profile is another characteristic cluster. Very often his literacy will not develop as effortlessly and automatically as you might expect – but his most obvious feature is likely to be his rather obsessive and eccentric personality. He is the perfectionist who gets very rattled by the unexpected, and who seems to take forever over his work, probably because of this obsessive need for order and perfection. He can be a bit clumsy, and his handwriting is poor, and his spelling and reading are not strong. But most obvious is his lack of social and interpersonal awareness, and his apparent difficulty in understanding how other people think. He comes across as an unhappy loner.

As well as literacy difficulties, what might be the three key clues as to the precise nature of his difficulty? He may

- **have a slightly odd way of talking – unusual intonation and prosody**
- **talk over others, or talk *at* them rather than *with* them – he'll seem to have no clue about the give-and-take nature of ordinary conversation and its rules**
- **take everything very literally, so that humour and metaphor pass right over his head, leaving him confused and defensive**

This is the way he *is*, and the best you can do will be to help him understand himself so that he can manage himself and his way of being, in ways that let him fit in better. Once that's in hand, then it will make every sense to help him to develop his literacy skills, or to compensate for them.

Clearly then, we have some fairly similar base ingredients for most of these children – but each with some key ingredients that make every one so very different from the other.

PART 2

How to identify specific learning difficulties

Identifying strands of difficulty: the wide-angle, then the in-depth

So how can you *use* all this information when you're trying to understand a particular child's learning difficulty?

One key message is *Don't look for single-label answers.* If you do, you'll have no problem finding one, and everyone will be happier – but it may be tunnel vision, and it may cause you to miss key information.

Starting with the wide angle

What do the clusters tell us about the first questions to be asked? Probably you already know quite a lot about this child, and probably some or all of the 'usual suspects' are evident: poor reading and spelling, dreadful handwriting, not a happy child, sometimes defiant, sometimes withdrawn, sometimes the clown, and *not* good at staying on task....

Your first reaction might be to find out more about those reading, spelling and handwriting problems, and see what you can do to help. But the clusters warn us that maybe there's more to this than meets the eye – the five key clusters described above suggest five initial key questions. As well as the most obvious questions, you need to ask:

CLUSTER 1: Does this learner seem a bit like John S, the classic 'phonological dyslexic'?

If so, do processing sounds, speech and spoken language seem to be a problem?

Does he...	**If so, have a closer look at**
<ul><li>forget or confuse what people say?</li><li>show perceptible delays in reaction times – e.g. hesitations and pauses in replying to questions?</li><li>have difficulty in finding the words he wants when talking – i.e. he knows what he wants to say but has difficulty/delay in putting it into words?</li></ul>	<ul><li>Phonological difficulties</li><li>Working memory</li><li>Processing speed</li><li>Expressive and receptive language disorders</li></ul> **as well as the more obvious core skills difficulties.**

CLUSTER 2: Does this learner seem a bit like Jenny J, the 'visual dyslexic'?

If so, are there signs of any visual discomfort or stress?

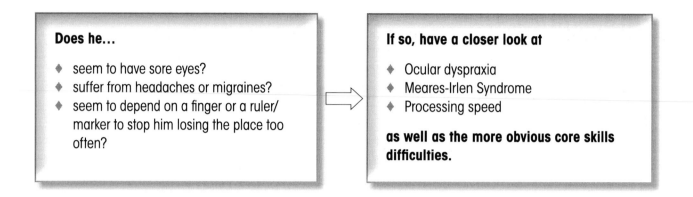

Does he...

- seem to have sore eyes?
- suffer from headaches or migraines?
- seem to depend on a finger or a ruler/ marker to stop him losing the place too often?

If so, have a closer look at

- Ocular dyspraxia
- Meares-Irlen Syndrome
- Processing speed

as well as the more obvious core skills difficulties.

CLUSTER 3: Does this learner seem a bit like Suzi M, the dyspraxic child?

Is there evidence of disorganisation, clumsiness and poor fine motor skills?

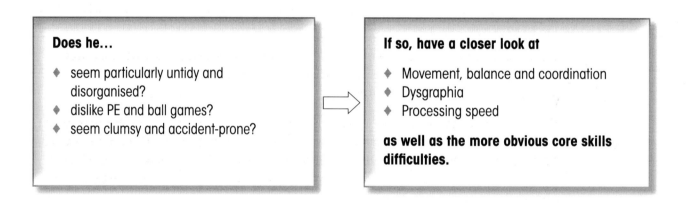

Does he...

- seem particularly untidy and disorganised?
- dislike PE and ball games?
- seem clumsy and accident-prone?

If so, have a closer look at

- Movement, balance and coordination
- Dysgraphia
- Processing speed

as well as the more obvious core skills difficulties.

CLUSTER 4: Does this learner seem a bit like Eric S, the hyperactive and inattentive lad?

Are over-activity, restlessness or inattention obvious features?

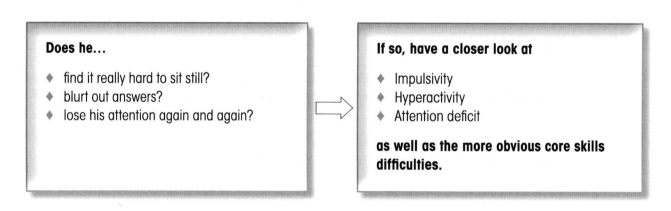

Does he...

- find it really hard to sit still?
- blurt out answers?
- lose his attention again and again?

If so, have a closer look at

- Impulsivity
- Hyperactivity
- Attention deficit

as well as the more obvious core skills difficulties.

CLUSTER 5: Does this learner seem a bit like Ahmed R, the boy with Asperger-like behaviours?

Does he seem somehow a bit different and eccentric, a bit out-of-kilter with the world around him?

Does he...	**If so, have a closer look at**
◆ hate change and cling to routines? ◆ have no idea about how to make and retain friends? ◆ talk *at* people, rather than with them, often boring his listener with an obsessive amount of information?	◆ Social awareness and communicative disorders ◆ Sensory integration difficulties and sensitivities **as well as the more obvious core skills difficulties.**

The answers to these questions should help you focus in – help you decide which strands you might usefully include in your assessment. They *may* not – learning difficulties are often infuriatingly elusive and hard to classify – but hopefully some of the answers will give you *some* kind of a hunch about which strands to look at in more depth, and how to look at them.

That's what the rest of this Part is about. It takes each of the strands in turn, each potential component of a child's difficulties, and sets out the kinds of questions you need to ask, the kind of evidence you need to gather.

The answers to the five key questions you've already asked should let you home in quickly and effectively, and make an effective decision about which clusters and strands you need to look at more closely. The rest of Part 2 tells you how to *identify* each of eighteen potential contributory strands; and then Part 3 sets out how to *respond* to each of them.

You have to decide just *which* strands merit closer inspection – that can be a difficult call, and you're the only person who can make it. The computer-aided **Special Needs Assessment Profile (SNAP-SpLD)** (Weedon, C. & Reid, G., Version 3.5, Hodder Education, 2012) can go a *long* way towards doing it for you – but arguably no package can improve upon the informed judgement of the professional on the ground. Making that informed judgement, then acting upon it, is what this book helps you do.

Once you've decided what is most important to look at, for a particular learner, use the following pages for detailed advice about how to assess for and identify each of the strands you want to explore. For each of the eighteen strands, there are

1. **Questions you need to ask,** and

2. **Tests and tasks that offer insights,** where such tests are appropriate for use in school.

A few selected tests are described, where appropriate, for most of the strands – tests that are reasonably priced and aimed at use within schools. The ones described are those familiar to the author, and include some 'composite' tests, or test batteries, that explore a range of characteristics of SpLDs – but obviously, other tests are available, some perhaps already in use in your school, and there's no reason not to use these tests if they tell you what you need to know.

The composite test kits are the **Dyslexia Portfolio** and the **Dyslexia Screening Tests**. Kits of this nature are not cheap, but they are wide-ranging and enduring, and they give you an enormous amount of what you need to know. There are as well some **SNAP-SpLD** 'probes', provided in Appendix 3, that may be helpful.

The photocopiable **Assessment Checklist and Outcomes** record sheet in Appendix 1 guides you through the process with:

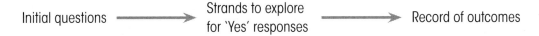

Initial questions ⟶ Strands to explore for 'Yes' responses ⟶ Record of outcomes

Appendix 2 shows a completed sample. The first sheet guides you through the questions you need to ask and the strands you'll want to follow up. The second sheet gives you a summary of your finding for each child, showing which strands are likely to be a **mild/moderate/significant** barrier to his learning, and gives you a steer about whether or not this might need onward referral and SEN status.

The first part of the completed checklist, for a hypothetical ten-year-old Tomas, with some dyslexic and dyspraxic difficulties, is shown below (see Appendix 2 for Tomas' full record and profile).

Record Sheet 1: SpLD Assessment Checklist and Outcomes

Pupil name	Date of assessment	Age at assessment	Assessing teacher/staff member
Tomes Linden	03/04/12	10 years 3 months	Amy Wainwright

Initial questions ⟹ **Strands to explore for 'Yes' responses** ⟹ **Record of outcomes**

Initial questions for Cluster 1 ('phonological dyslexic')

As well as some difficulties with core skills, does s/he...	Yes or No
● Forget or confuse what people say?	Yes
● Show perceptible delays in reaction times – replying to questions; hesitations and pauses?	
● Have difficulty in finding the words s/he wants when talking – i.e. knows what he/she wants to say but has difficulty/delay in putting it into words?	

Initial questions for Cluster 2 ('visual dyslexic')

As well as some difficulties with core skills, does s/he...	Yes or No
● Seem to have sore eyes?	No
● Suffer from headaches or migraines?	
● Seem to depend on a finger or a ruler/marker to stop him/her losing the place too often?	

Reading difficulties
Spelling difficulties
Dyscalculia
Dysgraphia
Phonological difficulties
Auditory processing difficulties
Working memory
Processing speed
Expressive and receptive language disorders
Deficiency in essential fatty acids

Reading difficulties
Spelling difficulties
Dyscalculia
Dysgraphia
Visual tracking and ocular control
Meares-Irlen Syndrome
Processing speed

Strand of difficulty	Strands to explore	Need identified? Yes/No
Processing Speed difficulties	✓	Yes
Working Memory difficulties	✓	No
Movement, Balance, Coordination and Planning difficulties	✓	Yes
Sensory Integration Difficulties and Sensitivities		

And this is how the second sheet might look:

Record Sheet 2: The 'Yes' responses
Profile arising from record of outcomes

Name Tomas Linden			Date 03/04/12	
Strand of difficulty	**Strands where need identified**	**Evidence and/or test scores**	**Strands suggesting possible SEN**	**Level of need:** **Mild/** **Moderate/** **Significant**
Processing Speed difficulties	Yes	Slightly below average single-word reading speed and 1 min writing on DST; very low PhAB naming Speed	SpLD Dyslexia	Moderate
Working Memory difficulties				
Movement, Balance, Coordination and Planning difficulties	Yes	SNAP balancing task hard, and parental and teacher reports of clumsiness, and poor fine coordination	SpLD Dyspraxia	Moderate
Sensory Integration Difficulties and Sensitivities			SpLD Dyspraxia and/or ASD/Asperger's	
Autistic Spectrum Disorders/Asperger's Syndrome.			ASD/Asperger's	
Dysgraphia	Yes	Poor and slow handwriting, though legible, and found SNAP Figuree copying task very hard.	SpLD Dysgraphia	Moderate
Dyscalculia.			SpLD Dyscalulia	
Spelling difficulties	Yes	Standardised score of 78 on Dyslexia Portfolio Spelling; spelling very erratic and uncertain, and far below the level expected from the high quality of his ideas for writing	SpLD Dyslexia	Significant
Reading difficulties	Yes	Standardised score of 81 on Dyslexia Portfolio single-word reading – though comprehension better, if he has as much time as he needs	SpLD Dyslexia	Significant
Phonological difficulties				
Auditory Processing difficulties				
Meares-Irlen syndrome				
Visual Tracking and Ocular Control				
Expressive and Receptive Language disorders			Specific Language Disorders	

Focusing in: in-depth assessment for each strand ———

2.1 Identifying Processing Speed Difficulties

Questions you need to ask for Processing Speed Difficulties

- ◆ Is his reading obviously slow?
- ◆ Does he take longer than might be expected to copy text?
- ◆ Does he take longer than expected to complete written work?
- ◆ Are there perceptible delays in reaction times – e.g. hesitations and pauses in replying to questions, or difficulty in finding the words he wants when talking?

If your answer to some of these is Yes (and it may well be: processing speed difficulties are a significant strand for many learners), then some of the measures described here should give you more information about whether it is a significant barrier for this child.

Tests and tasks that offer insights into Processing Speed Difficulties

Reading speed measures

Some learners might be fine on reading tests like single-word reading, or reading comprehension, or non-word reading. Tests like these are usually **untimed**. Give them one of these tests and they may score at a level that suggests no obvious barrier.

But give them a **timed** reading test, and their scores may be obviously lower. The underlying mechanics of reading may have been sound enough to allow a child to cope with curricular demands up to a certain point – but with the approach of the exam years comes an increasing demand for reading effectively at speed. Reading tests with a **timed** dimension are the only way to gain insight into this. Here are some of them:

Test	Age range	What it comprises	Comments	Publisher
Hodder Oral Reading Tests – Reading speed	5 to 16+	The number of phonically regular short words that can be read in 60 seconds	Quick and simple insight into fluency and ease of simple decoding	Hodder Education
Wordchains	7+ years	Marking boundaries between strings of letters and then strings of words within a time limit	Allows speed of word recognition to be compared with speed of letter recognition	GL Assessment
Dyslexia Screening Test (Junior) – one-minute reading	6.6 to 11.5	Number of single words read in one minute	Quick and simple insight into fluency and ease of word reading Results suggest 'level of difficulty' rather than standardised scores	Pearson

Test	Age range	What it comprises	Comments	Publisher
Dyslexia Screening Test (Senior) – one-minute reading	11.6 to 16.5	Number of single words read in one minute	Quick and simple insight into fluency and ease of word reading Results suggest 'level of difficulty' rather than standardised scores	Pearson
Dyslexia Portfolio test of reading speed	6 to 16	Making Yes/No decisions about silently read statements within a time limit	Involves some comprehension as well as decoding/word recognition	GL Assessment
York Assessment of Reading Comprehension (YARC) – separate Primary and Secondary tests	5 to 16	Passage-reading fluency and rate (at the same time as comprehension)	Combines insights into reading accuracy, reading rate, and reading comprehension	GL Assessment

Writing speed measures

Most tests, exams and assessments have a time limit. A test may *intend* to measure, say, knowledge of the US political system, or the effects of global warming – but if the candidate has to write about it within a time limit, then it will often measure writing speed too. And that makes it an invalid test if the learner has a writing speed difficulty, however expert he is on the topic being tested. You need some reliable insight about how his speed of writing matches up to his other skills. Here are some assessments:

Test	Age range	What it comprises	Comments	Publisher
Handwriting Speed Assessment	11 to 16	20-minute piece of free writing	Free access Measures speed of generating extended prose	distributed by Patoss www.patoss-dyslexia.org
Dyslexia Portfolio tests of free writing or copying	6 to 16	Speed of free writing (or copying, for younger children)	Free writing is a sentence-completion task, so does not probe generating extended prose	GL Assessment
Dyslexia Screening Test (Junior) – one-minute writing	6.6 to 11.5	Number of words copied in one minute	No composing skills involved, only speed of word formation	Pearson
Dyslexia Screening Test (Senior) – one-minute writing	11.6 to 16.5	Number of words copied in one minute	No composing skills involved, only speed of word formation	Pearson
DASH (Detailed Assessment of Speed of Handwriting)	9 to 16 (with 17+ version available)	Five subtests, each testing a different aspect of handwriting speed. The subtests examine fine motor and precision skills, the speed of producing well known symbolic material, the ability to alter speed of performance on two tasks with identical content and free-writing competency.	Very rigorous and extensive Perhaps expensive for in-school use	Pearson

Rapid naming measures

'Rapid Naming' is something that seems to be closely linked to specific barriers to learning, though it's hard to say just why. Sometimes known as RAN ('Rapid Automated Naming'), it involves simply measuring the time taken to give names to a sequence of pictures on the page. When you try it on yourself, you may find you're listening to yourself saying the wrong word, or suddenly finding that no word comes, even though you know *exactly* what you want to say. It gives you some insight into that word-finding difficulty that some pupils have, that apparent slowness and difficulty in accessing words and ideas that are clear as a bell to you, but somehow dodge out of reach as you try to get at them. Here are some tests:

Test	Age range	What it comprises	Comments	Publisher
SNAP-SpLD Picture Naming	5 to 14	Time taken to name pictures	Free, but not fully standardised – a very approximate measure	Hodder Education – see Appendix 3
Phonological Assessment Battery (PhAB) – Rapid Naming Pictures	6 to 14	Time taken to name pictures	Simple, easy to administer, yields standardised score	GL Assessment
Dyslexia Portfolio – Naming Speed	6 to 16	Time taken to name pictures	Simple, easy to administer, yields standardised score	GL Assessment
Dyslexia Screening Test (Junior) – Rapid Naming	6.6 to 11.5	Time taken to name pictures	Simple, easy to administer Results suggest 'level of difficulty' rather than standardised scores	Pearson
Dyslexia Screening Test (Senior) – Rapid Naming	11.6 to 16.5	Time taken to name pictures	Simple, easy to administer Results suggest 'level of difficulty' rather than standardised scores	Pearson

2.2 Identifying Working Memory Difficulties

Questions you need to ask for Working Memory Difficulties

- Does he have difficulty remembering a sequence of instructions, and need to have just one bit of information at a time?
- Does he seem inattentive?
- Does he forget recent events, or find it hard to hold in mind the information he needs while working at something?
- Does he seem to lose track of his own train of thought?
- Does he struggle with taking down information or making notes, and need to go much more slowly than you'd expect?
- Is mental arithmetic especially hard for him?
- Does he make spelling errors where the right letters are there, but in the wrong order?

If your answer to some of these is Yes, then some of the measures described here should give you more information about whether it is a significant barrier for this child. Working memory difficulties can be with auditory memory or with visual memory.

A note of caution: apparently similar tasks from different test batteries sometimes give conflicting results, and it's hard to say why. It may be that performance on working memory tasks is easily affected by other factors, so it may be useful to repeat the task another day. (The nature of these tasks means that practice effect is not likely to affect the results.)

Tests and tasks that offer insights into Working Memory Difficulties

Test	Age range	What it comprises	Comments	Publisher
SNAP-SpLD Backward Span	5 to 14	Recall of heard words	Free, but not fully standardised – a very approximate measure	Hodder Education – see Appendix 3
SNAP-SpLD Visual memory	5 to 14	Recall of visual information	Free, but not fully standardised – a very approximate measure	Hodder Education – see Appendix 3
Dyslexia Screening Test (Junior) – backward digit span	6.6 to 11.5	Repeating spoken numbers in reverse order	Simple, easy to administer Results suggest 'level of difficulty' rather than standardised scores Measures only backward span	Pearson
Dyslexia Screening Test (Senior) – backward digit span	11.6 to 16.5	Repeating spoken numbers in reverse order	Simple, easy to administer Results suggest 'level of difficulty' rather than standardised scores Measures only backward span	Pearson
Dyslexia Portfolio – Recall of Digits	6 to 16	Memorising and manipulating lists of digits (auditory memory)	Simple, easy to administer, yields standardised score, and explores both forward and backward span	GL Assessment

2.3 Identifying Spelling Difficulties

Questions you need to ask for Spelling Difficulties

- Is his spelling obviously less well developed than you might expect?
- Does he seem to be able to spell well enough in a spelling test, when spelling has his full attention, but spell noticeably less well when he is writing, when less attention is available for spelling?
- Does his spelling of the same word vary erratically within the same piece of writing, or from day to day?
- Can he learn a spelling list well enough, but appear to forget it very quickly?
- Does he appear to have little visual memory of a spelling, depending instead on phonic skills that are not helpful with sight words and irregular spellings?

If your answer to some of these is Yes, then some of the measures described here should give you more information about whether it is a significant barrier for this child.

Tests and tasks that offer insights into Spelling Difficulties

Test	Age range	What it comprises	Comments	Publisher
Graded Word Spelling Test	5 to 18+	80 test words, graded in order of difficulty – a revised and re-standardised version of the Vernon word spelling test	Wide age range, well known, and easy to administer	Hodder Education
Dyslexia Portfolio – Single-word Spelling	6 to 16	List of single words, graded for difficulty	Simple, easy to administer, yields standardised score	GL Assessment
Dyslexia Screening Test (Junior) – two-minute spelling	6.6 to 11.5	List of single words, graded for difficulty, within a time limit	Simple, easy to administer Results suggest 'level of difficulty' rather than standardised scores	Pearson
Dyslexia Screening Test (Senior) – two-minute spelling	11.6 to 16.5	List of single words, graded for difficulty, within a time limit	Simple, easy to administer Results suggest 'level of difficulty' rather than standardised scores	Pearson
SWST (Single-word Spelling Test)	6 to 14	Nine standardised tests, each with 30–50 words from everyday vocabulary	Available in paper and digital forms	GL Assessment

2.4 Identifying Reading Difficulties

Questions you need to ask for Reading Difficulties

- Is his oral reading inaccurate, or noticeably slow and laborious?
- Does he fear having to read aloud in front of others?
- Does he simply not seem to understand text that you'd have expected him to understand?
- When reading aloud, does he not seem to notice when he's read something wrong, something that doesn't fit or make sense?
- Is there a multi-tasking issue, so that he can read aloud reasonably well, but not apparently be able to *process* the meaning at the same time? Or conversely, can he take in the meaning well enough when reading silently, but not if he has to allocate attention at the same time to orally decoding and articulating the passage?

If your answer to some of these is Yes, then some of the measures described here should give you more information about whether it is a significant barrier for this child.

Reading is certainly the most important single literacy skill, and a very complex one. You need to be clear in your mind just what you learn from scores on different kinds of reading tests. It's perhaps useful to simplify the complexity into a few broad areas:

- the ability to *decode* phonically regular words, and phonically irregular words (sight words);
- the *fluency* and *speed* of doing so, and the *accuracy*;
- the changing-up of gear needed when doing so with *prose* rather than single words;
- the ability to multi-task, so that decoding the text doesn't take all the available attention, but enough is left over to take in the *meaning* of the text at the same time (it is very usual for some dyslexics to come a cropper with this: they can read aloud OK, or they can read silently and have a fair idea what it's saying – but ask them to do both at once and there's just not enough attentional resource available);
- the metacognitive ability to self-monitor, and recognise that the word you thought you've just read doesn't make sense, so that you return to it and try again;
- the extra attentional resource and language skills needed to go beyond literal comprehension – the noting of the factual information – to inferencing, and 'reading between the lines'.

These broad areas probably sum up the constituent skills for the normally developing reader – but personal style impacts too. Some of us instinctively attend to detail when reading (those irritating colleagues who like to point up your typos in work you checked carefully, typos that no one else noticed either); others of us lean more towards skimming for meaning – we're good at getting the gist, but we may miss some minor points.

And obviously, too, where there are any learning difficulties, co-morbidity needs to be kept in mind: the ASD child isn't going to infer naturally when reading (they tend to be very literal in all their thinking); the child with working memory or attentional difficulties isn't going to find it easy to monitor emerging meaning and self-correct; the 'hyperlexic' child may be swift and accurate at decoding and reading aloud expressively and well, but not have much of a clue what it's about.

The first of the measures below focus upon the core skills of decoding and word recognition; the latter tests include comprehension. When you use them – or any others – do keep in mind all this complexity: reading is not a unitary skill!

Tests and tasks that offer insights into Reading Difficulties

Test	Age range	What it comprises	Comments	Publisher
Decoding and single-word reading				
Dyslexia Portfolio – single-word reading	6 to 16	Speed of reading aloud single words of increasing difficulty	Allows comparison of reading *ability* and *speed* (adjacent tests in same battery)	GL Assessment
Dyslexia Screening Test (Junior) – one-minute reading	6.6 to 11.5	List of single words, graded for difficulty, within a time limit	Simple, easy to administer Results suggest 'level of difficulty' rather than standardised scores	Pearson
Dyslexia Screening Test (Senior) – one-minute reading	11.6 to 16.5	List of single words, graded for difficulty, within a time limit	Simple, easy to administer Results suggest 'level of difficulty' rather than standardised scores	Pearson
Comprehension				
Diagnostic Reading Analysis	7 to 16	Oral reading and questions on graded passages,	Wide age range, easy to administer, suitable for less confident readers	Hodder Education
Hodder Oral Reading Tests	5 to 16	Test reading comprehension at word, sentence and continuous text levels	Wide age range, easy to administer	Hodder Education
York Assessment of Reading Comprehension	4 to 16	Tests of comprehension, accuracy and fluency	Different approaches depending upon age; but all allow comparison between accuracy, speed and comprehension	GL Assessment

2.5 Identifying Dyscalculia

Questions you need to ask for Dyscalculia

◆ Does he find it hard to remember number facts, the kinds of things that should be coming automatically?
◆ Is mental arithmetic especially hard for him?
◆ Does he get confused by simple mathematical symbols and what they mean?
◆ Is telling the time unduly hard for him?
◆ Does there seem to be much less sense of money than you'd expect – e.g. he has no idea how much change to expect from a simple transaction; or gives erratic or bizarre answers to simple money problems?
◆ Does he tend to miscount a lot?

If your answer to some of these is Yes, then some of the measures described here should give you more information about whether it is a significant barrier for this child. There are few tests aimed *specifically* at identifying dyscalculia – more often you will be alerted by scores on other maths or arithmetic tests that are clearly lower than you'd expect from performance on other tasks. Whether being 'always bad at maths' is different from being 'dyscalculic' probably isn't too important – you're arguably more concerned with effects rather than causes. The child who's having to count on his fingers while processing a formula in a physics problem isn't getting a fair chance to show how good a physicist he is. That's why poor number grasp can be disabling, and needs to be pinned down and recognised. Probably your school already tracks maths and number attainment for every pupil, and those scores may well tell you what you need to know.

Tests and tasks that offer insights into Dyscalculia

Test	Age range	What it comprises	Comments	Publisher
Dyscalculia Screener	6 to 14	Computer assessment of reaction time, number awareness and arithmetical skills	Comprehensive, and focused on underlying attributes such as reaction time and number awareness rather than just level of attainment in skills that have been taught	GL Assessment
MaLT – Mathematics Assessment for Learning and Teaching	4 to 15	Paper and pencil tests, whole class or individual	Wide age range, and easy to administer Diagnostic error analysis Onscreen computer-adaptive version includes audio support and automatic timing of responses	Hodder Education

Test	Age range	What it comprises	Comments	Publisher
Access Mathematics Tests 1 and 2	Test 1 for 7 to 12; Test 2 for 11 to 16+	Mainly open-ended questions presented in order of difficulty Parallel forms A and B for both tests	Provide a skills profile and a standardised total score	Hodder Education
Basic Number Screening Test	7 to 12	Identifies pupils with low number attainment	Verbally delivered, and no reading required; recently restandardised	Hodder Education
Basic Number Diagnostic Test	5 to 7	Profiles key aspects of developing numeracy to identify potential difficulties	Useful for early years, with emphasis upon number skills attainment	Hodder Education

An informal task that gives you some insight into a pupil's underlying **sense of number** is simply to show him a straight line on a sheet of plain paper. Tell him that **zero** is at the left-hand end, and **ten** is at the right-hand end, even though there are no numbers shown on the sheet of paper.

Then ask him to point to where on the line he'd expect **seven** to be. Most children can do this easily. If he can't make a fair approximation, then he lacks even the most basic sense of number, and his dyscalculic difficulty is likely to be profound, and go well beyond the more typical difficulty in accessing number facts.

2.6 Identifying Deficiencies of Essential Fatty Acids

Questions you need to ask for Deficiencies of Essential Fatty Acids (or, more probably, questions you need to ask his parents...)

- Does he seem unusually thirsty, or need to urinate rather often?
- Does he have rather rough, dry or scaly skin?
- Is his hair a bit dull, dry or lifeless looking?
- Does he have dandruff?
- Does he have soft or brittle nails?
- Are there raised bumps on the skin (usually of outer arm)?
- Is he prone to allergic tendencies (eczema, asthma, hayfever, etc)?

If your answer to some of these is Yes, then some dietary supplement may well be helpful – see section 3.6.

At the time of writing, there are no tests or tasks that offer insights into Deficiencies of Essential Fatty Acids that can be carried out in school – if confirmation is wanted, then suggest a GP referral. But probably this isn't necessary – the supplements are available through high-street pharmacies, and most families go ahead on a *'Let's try it and see'* basis... nothing to be lost, and perhaps something to be gained.

Obviously, some of these manifestations can be symptoms of more serious underlying disorders – thirst and frequent urination might be linked to diabetes, for example – so it may be worth considering a GP referral anyway if any of these indicators are most unusually prominent.

Obviously, too, a fatty acid deficit may be due to an individual's inability to metabolise specific nutrients – the nutrients are there in the diet, but not being taken up and utilised efficiently, so that supplements might help – or it may be down to wider dietary issues, in which case his whole diet needs to be considered. Distinguishing between these goes well beyond the classroom and our remit and expertise as teachers – but insights from parents/carers may provide a useful steer.

Again, section 3.6 should help point up the best way forward.

2.7 Identifying Phonological Difficulties

Questions you need to ask for Phonological Difficulties

- ◆ Did he find it hard to learn the names and sounds of letters?
- ◆ Does he find it hard to decode a word a sound at a time?
- ◆ Does he sometimes omit vowels when spelling words?
- ◆ Does he sometimes confuse the sounds within words when speaking, such as 'aminal', 'hostipal', etc?
- ◆ Does he have difficulty pronouncing new words and remembering them?
- ◆ Does he sometimes omit sounds from spoken words?
- ◆ Does he sometimes mispronounce frequently-occurring words?
- ◆ Do his parents report any history of glue ear?
- ◆ Did he not enjoy or struggle with rhymes, word games, or have difficulty recognising words that start with the same sound?

If your answer to some of these is Yes, then some of the measures described here should give you more information about whether it is a significant barrier for this child.

Tests and tasks that offer insights into Phonological Difficulties

Test	Age range	What it comprises	Comments	Publisher
Dyslexia Screening Test (Junior) Phonemic segmentation Rhyme	6.6 to 11.5	Identifying and manipulating the constituent sounds within words Ability with rhyming sounds	Simple, easy to administer Results suggest 'level of difficulty' rather than standardised scores	Pearson
Dyslexia Screening Test (Senior) Phonemic segmentation Rhyme	11.6 to 16.5	Identifying and manipulating the constituent sounds within words Ability with rhyming sounds	Simple, easy to administer Results suggest 'level of difficulty' rather than standardised scores	Pearson
Dyslexia Portfolio – phoneme deletion	6 to 16	Identifying and manipulating the constituent sounds within words	Simple, easy to administer Gives standardised scores	GL Assessment
Dyslexia Portfolio – non-word reading	6 to 16	Ability to read pseudowords	Simple, easy to administer Gives standardised scores	GL Assessment
Phonological Assessment Battery – Alliteration Rhyme Spoonerisms	6 to 14	Ability to identify and manipulate initial sounds within words, process rhyme, and manipulate sequence of sounds within words	Three subtests from the same battery provide insights into different aspects of phonology	GL Assessment

2.8 Identifying Auditory Processing Difficulties

Questions you need to ask for Auditory Processing Difficulties

◆ Does he have difficulty in remembering or following a sequence of instructions?

◆ Does he seem to cope better with visually-presented information?

◆ Is there difficulty in listening when there are other noises or distractions, or background noise?

◆ Does he sometimes misperceive a word to be a similar-sounding word to that which was spoken?

◆ Does he appear to have poor listening skills, and need people to speak slowly?

◆ Is there an exaggerated reaction to loud noises?

◆ Do his parents report that he finds noisy environments (such as a busy shop or a party) specially hard?

◆ When he is concentrating on a task, is he easily put off by background noises?

◆ Does he ask for things to be repeated, or demonstrate that he might not have heard something properly?

If your answer to some of these is Yes, then there may well be some barriers that arise out of inefficient processing of sound and the spoken word. (This is *not* the same as *hearing* difficulties, or issues arising out of auditory *acuity*. It refers instead to inefficiencies in the ways sounds are processed once they have *been* heard.)

This is not something that can easily be explored further within the school, and referral to a speech and language therapist may be needed. Certainly, it will often be a good idea to have a hearing test before proceeding to auditory therapy, to rule out a conventional hearing difficulty/lack of acuity (as opposed to a difficulty in the ways words are processed once they have been heard). Alternatively, you or the family can find out more about the six main auditory training programmes used in the UK – four home-based and two centre-based – from these websites:

Programme	Home or centre-based	Website
Johansen	Home-based	www.johansenias.com
Samonas	Home-based	www.samonas.com
The Listening Programme	Home-based	www.thelisteningprogram.com
Tomatis Solisten	Home-based	www.solistentraining.com
The Tomatis Method	Centre-based	www.tomatis.com
Auditory Integration Training (AIT)	Centre-based	www.berardaitwebsite.com

2.9 Identifying Expressive and Receptive Language Disorders

Questions you need to ask for Expressive and Receptive Language Disorders

- ◆ Does he forget or confuse what people say?
- ◆ Do his parents report that he was late in starting to talk?
- ◆ Is his speech poorly articulated, slow, hesitant, confused, or poorly controlled?
- ◆ Does he have a stammer or stutter?
- ◆ Does he sometimes muddle and jumble words and grammar when speaking?
- ◆ Does he have difficulty in finding the words he wants when talking?
- ◆ Does he find it hard to plan what he wants to say – i.e. knows what is needed to be said but displays difficulty/delay in putting it into words?

Speech and language difficulties can be seen as having four main strands:

- ◆ **Speech** – the speech sounds we produce;
- ◆ **Grammar** – the way we put words together to form phrases and sentences;
- ◆ **Vocabulary and Semantics** – words and their meaning;
- ◆ **Pragmatics** – using language appropriately in different social situations.

Gaining a full picture of all of these is not something that can easily be done within the school, and referral to a speech and language therapist is needed if you think there are possibly significant difficulties. Shown below, though, are a few accessible and useful tests that probe vocabulary and word access/retrieval, which may help you judge whether a referral is justified.

Tests and tasks that offer insights into Expressive and Receptive Language Disorders

Test	Age range	What it comprises	Comments	Publisher
British Picture Vocabulary Scale	3 to 16	Choosing the correct picture to exactly match a spoken word	Easy to administer Gives useful insight into understanding the content of spoken language	GL Assessment
Dyslexia Screening Test (Junior) – Verbal fluency Semantic fluency Vocabulary	6.6 to 11.5	Speed of producing words that rhyme or alliterate Speed of producing words by semantic category Multiple-choice test of receptive vocabulary and reasoning ability	Three aspects of language are probed Results suggest 'level of difficulty' rather than standardised scores	Pearson
Dyslexia Screening Test (Senior) – Verbal fluency Semantic fluency	11.6 to 16.5	Speed of producing words that rhyme or alliterate Speed of producing words by semantic category	Three aspects of language are probed Results suggest 'level of difficulty' rather than standardised scores	Pearson

2.10 Identifying Meares–Irlen Syndrome

Questions you need to ask for Meares–Irlen Syndrome

- Does he blink excessively, grimace, or rub his/her eyes when reading?
- Does he complain of watery eyes, or hot/dry/sore eyes when reading?
- Does he report letters moving, jumping or blurring, or speak of 'rivers/snakes of white' in text?
- Does reading causes visual fatigue, headaches or migraines?
- Does he speak of seeing letters as 'jumbles of black marks on the page'?
- Is there an exaggerated reaction to very bright light or sunshine or a photo flash?

If your answer to some of these is Yes, then it may well be that this should be explored further by an optometrist (see www.college-optometrists.org to find a local optometrist) or an orthoptist, usually accessed via a medical/GP referral (see www.orthoptics.org.uk). The Crossbow package below may help.

Tests and tasks that offer insights into Meares–Irlen Syndrome

Age range	What it comprises	Comments	Publisher
All	The Visual Stress Assessment Pack from Crossbow Education includes assessment materials, coloured overlays, tinted rulers and writing paper, as well as a 'Find Your Local Visual Stress Specialist' option	Extremely wide-ranging and comprehensive	www.crossboweducation.com

Use of the kits like the *Visual Stress Assessment* pack may well allow you a pretty clear idea of what is going on – for example, if reading with a coloured overlay makes a really obvious difference, or using a tinted ruler means he suddenly stops losing his place, then you've gained an invaluable diagnostic insight, and onward referral to an optometrist or orthoptist is indicated if you want a fuller picture and an appropriately focused intervention.

Conversely, such packs may be most useful in *ruling out* the need for any further investigation – if these aids make absolutely no difference to his reading, then it is probably safe to assume that this kind of visual stress does not constitute a barrier to his learning.

2.11 Identifying Visual Stress and Ocular Control issues

Questions you need to ask for Visual Stress and Ocular Control issues

- Is he unusually dependent on using a finger or marker as a pointer when reading?
- Does he tend to jump lines, or repeat lines, when reading?
- Does he tend to miss out small words when reading?
- Does he have unusual posture when reading or writing, or sit an unusual distance from the text?

If your answer to some of these is Yes, then it may well be that this should be explored further by an optometrist (see www.college-optometrists.org to find a local optometrist) or an orthoptist, usually accessed via a medical/GP referral (see www.orthoptics.org.uk)

Tests and tasks that offer insights into Visual Stress and Ocular Control issues

Probably there are few ways of exploring this with any rigour in school, but there are some simple ways of gaining a little further insight about ocular control, and whether it seems to be a real problem that merits orthoptic or optometric assessment:

1. Hold a pencil in front of him, and move it slowly towards his nose. Ask him to say when it becomes a double image. Try it on a few other volunteers (children with no apparent difficulties), and compare the results – if it doubles when still well away from the nose, binocular control may be an issue.

2. Move a pencil back and forth in front of his eyes while he watches it. Do his eyes flicker or hesitate or lack smoothness of tracking, especially as the pencil crosses the midline?

3. Use a small hand mirror, and hold it so that you can watch his eyes while he reads. Does his tracking seem uncertain in any way? (Again, maybe try it on a few other volunteers – children with no apparent difficulties – and compare the results.)

Some of these are described in the **SNAP** probe shown in Appendix 3, and the Crossbow *Visual Stress Assessment Pack* may also be useful.

Test	Age range	What it comprises	Comments	Publisher
SNAP-SpLD – Vergence and visual tracking	5 to 14	Observing eye movements	Free and simple to use Approximate level of difficulty only – not standardised scores	Hodder Education – see Appendix 3
Visual Stress Assessment Pack	All	Includes assessment materials, coloured overlays, tinted rulers and writing paper, as well as a 'Find Your Local Visual Stress Specialist' option	Extremely wide-ranging and comprehensive	www. crossboweducation. com

2.12 Identifying Dysgraphia

Questions you need to ask for Dysgraphia

Dysgraphia often refers to a combination of spelling difficulties with handwriting and page presentation difficulties. Because spelling difficulties are dealt with separately, it refers here only to 'pure' dysgraphia – that is, difficulties with page presentation, organisation and handwriting.

◆ Are handwriting and page layout in general a problem?
◆ Is copying text from one place to another untidy and poorly laid out – e.g from text or board to notes or exercise book?
◆ Does he hold the pen or pencil in an awkward or unusual way?
◆ Is his handwriting rather illegible (in spite of trying hard)?
◆ Does he tend not to join up the letters when writing, or to favour upper case, or to mix upper and lower case?
◆ Does handwriting need a big effort and take a long time?
◆ Does he report pain in hand or arm when writing?
◆ Does he press too hard when writing?
◆ Is his letter formation rather odd or wrong-looking?

If your answer to the majority of these is Yes, and it's not just because he simply can't be bothered, then that's enough in itself. There are no realistic standardised tests that quantify dysgraphia, and your judgement is the key, so trust it! The **SNAP** probe given below and in Appendix 3 may be of some help, and you may have some similar tests somewhere at the back of your cupboard...:

Test	Age range	What it comprises	Comments	Publisher
SNAP-SpLD – Figure copying	5 to 14	Copying of shapes	Free and simple to use Approximate level of difficulty only – not standardised scores	Hodder Education – see Appendix 3
DASH (Detailed Assessment of Speed of Handwriting)	9 to 16 (with 17+ version available)	Five subtests, each testing a different aspect of handwriting speed. The subtests examine fine motor and precision skills, the speed of producing well-known symbolic material, the ability to alter speed of performance on two tasks with identical content and free-writing competency.	Very rigorous and extensive Perhaps expensive for in-school use	Pearson

2.13 Identifying Movement, Balance, Coordination and Planning Difficulties

Questions you need to ask for Movement, Balance, Coordination and Planning Difficulties

◆ Does he seem to have unusual difficulty with work that must be committed to paper, even though he can manage the ideas orally?

◆ Is he rather untidy looking – e.g. with clothes not fastened properly?

◆ Does he find it hard to form or sustain relationships with other children, and appear isolated in class and/or in the playground?

◆ Does he have difficulty in organising himself, and in organising tasks and activities, often losing and forgetting things?

◆ Does he find ball games hard?

◆ Does he find it hard to copy shapes?

◆ Are gait, posture or movements odd or slightly unusual in any way?

◆ Does he have difficulty using hand tools – e.g. scissors to cut out shapes neatly?

◆ Does he find PE lessons difficult, or not enjoy them?

◆ Does he sometimes appear clumsy or accident prone?

◆ Does it take longer than expected to learn a new physical activity?

◆ Did/are difficulties in dressing, tying shoelaces, etc, persist longer than would be expected?

And some things you might find out from his parents...

◆ Was the birth process prolonged, difficult or unusual in any way?

◆ Was the birth either very early or late?

◆ Did he miss going through the crawling stage (i.e. did he 'bum-shuffle' instead of crawl?)

◆ Was he late starting to walk?

◆ Was he reluctant to draw, colour or paint as a small child?

◆ Did it take an unusually long time to learn to use a knife and fork in a coordinated way?

These are characteristics that are often lumped together under the heading of **developmental coordination disorder**, or more often **dyspraxia** – a word maybe worth treating cautiously, because parents Google it and frighten themselves, usually unnecessarily. These kinds of difficulties can sometimes be elusive and apparently unconvincing – *'He's a good football player....'* or *'He's always loved Lego... so how can he be* **dyspraxic**?*'* – and it does often seem a bit counter-intuitive to suggest it. But that's the way it seems to be: someone can be very uncoordinated and physically inefficient and disorganised with some skills, while quite impressive with others.

So don't expect Yes to be the answer to all, or even most, of these questions. If Yes is the answer to even a significant minority, it's certainly worth pursuing further. If the difficulty seems significant, refer onwards for assessment by an occupational therapist or movement specialist: while the tests listed below allow you some glimpses and insights, most of the more rigorous assessment instruments need to be administered by a qualified health professional or specialist agency. But, more likely, trust your own judgement, and if you're seeing a lot of these characteristic behaviours, assume and accept that this *is* a barrier for this learner. The tests below may help you decide about onward referral, but they are pretty approximate measures.

Tests and tasks that offer insights into Movement, Balance, Coordination and Planning difficulties

Test	Age range	What it comprises	Comments	Publisher
Dyslexia Screening Test (Junior) – Bead threading Postural stability	6.6 to 11.5	Speed of threading beads Maintaining balance when nudged	Results suggest 'level of difficulty' rather than standardised scores Balance task very approximate	Pearson
Dyslexia Screening Test (Senior) – Bead threading Postural stability	11.6 to 16.5	Speed of threading beads Maintaining balance when nudged	Results suggest 'level of difficulty' rather than standardised scores Balance task very approximate	Pearson
SNAP-SpLD – Balancing task	5 to 14	Maintaining balance while carrying out another cognitive task	Free and simple to use Approximate level of difficulty only – not standardised scores	Hodder Education – see Appendix 3
SNAP-SpLD – Bilateral integration	5 to 14	Drawing task that requires integration of left and right components	Free and simple to use Approximate level of difficulty only – not standardised scores	Hodder Education – see Appendix 3

2.14 Identifying Attention Deficit Disorder

Questions you need to ask for Attention Deficit Disorder

- Does he have difficulty remembering and following a sequence of instructions?
- Does he seem to need one-to-one instruction if he is to succeed – i.e. he can cope with the material, but seems to need to have each task explained individually before starting?
- Does he tend to leave tasks and activities unfinished, unless supervised?
- Does he seem not to listen or follow instructions unless his attention is captured first?
- Does he have difficulty in sustaining attention, or staying on task (except when really interested by something)?
- Is he easily distracted?
- Is he unusually forgetful?
- Is he easily bored?
- Does he make a lot of careless mistakes?
- Does he drift off into day dreams unusually easily?
- Does he sometimes seem very passive, and lacking any interests?

It's not realistic to try to *quantify* ADD with any kinds of standardised tests that are available to schools. Formal identification is ultimately a medical responsibility, and even here checklists rather than tests are usually used. So there are no 'tests and tasks' to suggest here.

We're all inattentive often enough – when we're bored, tired, distracted, hungry, anxious or stressed…. There are countless good reasons for drifting off-task, and we all do it sometimes. So keep that in mind when you're answering the questions, and don't answer 'Yes' if the inattention can be explained in some way.

But if it can't be explained, and if your answer to many of these is **'Yes, mildly or moderately so'**, make a note of that on Sheet 2 of the record form in Appendix 1, and go ahead and use any of the ideas and approaches in section 3.14 to help as best you can.

If your answer to many of them is **'Yes, significantly'**, and it's your hunch that an intrinsic inability to sustain attention and stay on-task is something that is really holding back this learner, then note that on his record sheet, and consider suggesting a GP referral as an initial step.

2.15 Identifying Hyperactive Difficulties

Questions you need to ask for Hyperactive Difficulties

- Does he talk excessively?
- Does he have difficulty in playing quietly?
- Does he tend to disturb other children?
- Does he seem to be in 'perpetual motion', squirming, fidgeting, tapping?
- Does he have difficulty remaining seated when expected?
- Does he run and climb excessively?
- Is he often 'on the go' or behaving as if 'driven by a motor'?

As with ADD, it's not realistic to try to *quantify* hyperactivity with any kinds of standardised tests that are available to schools. Formal identification is ultimately a medical responsibility, and even here checklists rather than tests are usually used. So there are no 'tests and tasks' to suggest here.

So if your answer to many of these is **'Yes, mildly or moderately so'**, make a note of that on Sheet 2 of the record form in Appendix 1, and go ahead and use any of the ideas and approaches in section 3.15 to help as best you can.

If your answer to many of them is **'Yes, significantly'**, and it's your hunch that an intrinsic inability to remain still and task-focused is something that is really holding back this learner, then note that on his record sheet, and consider suggesting a GP referral.

Before that, however, dietary issues may be worth considering, if only to rule them out. We've all seen children whose activity level is fine – until they have a particular fizzy drink, or kind of chocolate. Section 3.6 gives some useful references about diet that may be worth exploring if you want to rule out diet as a causal factor.

2.16 Identifying Impulsivity

Questions you need to ask for Impulsivity

- ◆ Does he blurt out answers, sometimes even before the question is completed?
- ◆ Does he tend not to foresee the consequence of an action?
- ◆ Does he find it hard to wait his turn?
- ◆ Does he often interrupt or intrude on others?
- ◆ Does he rush into things, without ever pausing to think it through at all?

As with hyperactivity (and most hyperactive kids will be impulsive ones too), it's just not realistic to try to *quantify* impulsivity with any kinds of standardised tests that are available to schools. Formal identification is ultimately a medical responsibility, and even here checklists rather than tests are usually used. So there are no 'tests and tasks' to suggest here.

So if your answer to many of these is **'Yes, mildly or moderately so'**, make a note of that on Sheet 2 of the record form in Appendix 1, and go ahead and use any of the ideas and approaches in section 3.16 to help as best you can.

If your answer to many of them is **'Yes, significantly'**, and it's your hunch that an intrinsic inability to control his own impulses is something that is really holding back this learner, then note that on his record sheet, and consider suggesting a GP referral as an initial step. Very often, there will be hyperactivity as well.

2.17 Identifying Sensory Integration Difficulties and Sensitivities

Questions you need to ask for Sensory Integration Difficulties and Sensitivities

- Are there exaggerated reactions to the texture of certain fabrics, or the texture of certain foods?
- Are there exaggerated reactions to some grooming activities, such as hair washing or nail cutting?
- Does he over-react to strongly flavoured food?
- Does he over-react to strong smells?
- Does he find things like swinging or spinning (e.g. at a fair or playground) obviously unpleasant?
- Are there exaggerated reactions to heights (e.g. going up a ladder)?
- Are there obvious over- or under-reactions to being touched, pushed or nudged?
- Are there exaggerated reactions to having his eyes closed or covered?
- Are there exaggerated reactions to rough and tumble play – e.g. jumping, pushing, banging, bouncing, etc?

Again, and as with ADHD traits, schools aren't in a position to try to *quantify* these kinds of sensitivities. They are often found where there are dyspraxic/ DCD issues, and in pupils on the autistic spectrum. They come more into the remit of health professionals, and even here checklists rather than tests are usually used. So there are no 'tests and tasks' to suggest here.

So if your answer to many of these is **'Yes, mildly or moderately so'**, make a note of that on Sheet 2 of the record form in Appendix 1, and go ahead and use any of the ideas and approaches in section 3.17 to help as best you can.

If your answer to many of them is **'Yes, significantly'**, and it's your hunch that these characteristics loom large in this child's life, and are linked to the barriers that may be holding back his learning, then note that on his record sheet, and consider suggesting a GP referral as an initial step, or an occupational therapist.

2.18 Identifying Social Awareness and Communicative Disorders

Questions you need to ask for Social Awareness and Communicative Disorders

- Is his speech odd-sounding, with unusual patterns of stress/intonation, or monotone?
- Does he have difficulty in taking part in conversations, and following its 'rules', listening to others, etc?
- Does he seem dependent on certain routines, and/or become unduly distressed by change – e.g. needs to be told well in advance before any change of activity?
- Does he find it difficult to cope with losing games, or accepting their rules?
- Does he tend to be very literal, and not to recognise implied meanings – e.g. understand jokes or notice slight sarcasm or irony?
- Does he seem to gain particular satisfaction from repetitive activities?
- Does he seem to have unusually all-absorbing/obsessive interests?
- Does he appear rather eccentric, a little different from others of the same age?
- Does he seem more interested in objects than people?
- Does he tend to find imaginative or creative play quite hard?
- Can he be obsessively perfectionist about some things?
- Is he sometimes intensely interested in detail, while tending not to see the overall 'big' picture?
- Does he have difficulty in changing/adapting his behaviour to suit different situations?
- Does he find it hard to pick up on social cues, and 'read' social situations or to recognise the feelings of others?
- Does he tend to talk *at* people, rather than *with* them or *to* them?
- Is eye contact poor when people are talking to him?
- Does he find it hard to form or sustain relationships with other children and appear isolated in class and/or in the playground?
- Are gait, posture or movements odd or slightly unusual in any way?

'Social awareness and communicative disorders' is another way of describing behaviours we associate with the autistic spectrum. Schools need to be very cautious indeed about suggesting that a child is 'on the spectrum' and diagnosis is a medical responsibility – emphatically not something for us as teachers. ASD is so much in the public eye now (and usefully so) that we are perhaps a little too ready to turn to it. But most of us have some characteristics that fit the pattern, and being a bit eccentric is **not** a special need or an identifiable syndrome. Still, having some characteristics that are mildly or moderately characteristic of ASD *is* something we can recognise and respond to, in ways that can sometimes be very helpful. But it's not for us to try to *quantify* these kinds of characteristics – so once again, there are no 'tests and tasks' to draw upon.

So rely on the questions you've asked. If your answer to many of these is **'Yes, mildly or moderately so'**, make a note of that on Sheet 2 of the record form in Appendix 1, and go ahead and use any of the ideas and approaches in section 3.18 to help as best you can.

If your answer to many of them is **'Yes, significantly'**, and it's your hunch that these may be important factors in this child's life, then note that on his record sheet, and consider suggesting a GP referral as the first important step in engaging the medical profession.

PART 3

How to respond to specific learning difficulties

You've identified which strands of difficulty may be significant for the child you're considering. Next thing is to *do* something about it.

It's helpful to think of three different levels of response to any difficulty:

1. Seeking and hopefully addressing possible **underlying causes**;

2. Working directly on the underdeveloped skills – **remediating** the difficulty;

3. Accepting the difficulty, and focusing upon finding ways to minimise its impact, ways of **compensating** so that this pupil will still achieve despite the difficulty – **supporting strategies** for the classroom and the exam hall.

Obviously, too, **finding out more** about the barrier will be helpful for school staff and for families or carers.

For some strands and barriers, there will be useful things to do at all three levels. For others, it may be most important to focus on one of the levels much more than the others.

Sometimes this choice will be governed by the child's age and stage. For example, a 7-year-old with a significant spelling difficulty may well benefit from lots of work aimed at **remediating** the difficulty; but the same difficulty in a 17-year-old is best accepted and **compensated** for, by binning pen and paper and turning instead to computer with spellcheck for written work. That judgement call will be for you and the family to make, and your choices and emphases will shift as the child moves up the school.

In other cases, the nature of the difficulty, the nature of that particular barrier, will guide your choices. **Processing speed difficulties** (see below) are a good example of this. Sure, there may be packages and programmes out there that claim to make you think/read/write/reason/compute/analyse more quickly, and lots of electronic games must surely develop exactly these skills, so that you certainly get faster at that particular game or programme. You may well feel that you are addressing **underlying causes** and **remediating** at the same time, and perhaps you are to some extent. But it's less certain that it all transfers to the classroom and to academic work, and for difficulties like these it's probably best to accept them, and to **compensate** for them.

So, to each of the difficulties in turn (and all of these pages may be *photocopied for colleagues*)....

3.1 How do I respond to and support Processing Speed Difficulties?

This is the youngster who *can* do the thinking, who *can* complete the task – but who seems to take an unusual length of time to do so. **Addressing underlying causes** and **Remediating** are probably not realistic options for a processing speed difficulty *on its own* (though the difficulty may be diminished through some of the actions taken in responding to associated strands). For this particular strand of difficulty, better to focus instead on how to **compensate** for it, to make sure it doesn't stand in the way of this pupil doing as well as he should....

Compensating and supporting strategies

- Allow extra time for timed tasks, especially in assessments and examinations – but only if his teachers are sure that he really does need to have this extra time if he is to demonstrate his true level of attainment. The question is not *'Would he do better with extra time?'* Most of us would. The question is *'Does he score clearly below the level I know he should score, and it's not just because of poor time management?'*
  The obvious clues are unfinished answer papers; or sometimes answers that are much thinner than expected, because he's learned to pace himself and manage his time. It means he's not got enough time to show what he knows in the time allocated by the examiners.
- Consider a request to examination boards for extra time, if appropriate and required.
- Remind his teachers that copying and note-making, from the board or a textbook, may take longer than expected. This may mean giving him pre-prepared notes, or photocopies of another pupil's. (While there's maybe some truth in the idea that he'll absorb the ideas by having to write them down himself, it's more likely that he'll get seriously frustrated as well as ending up with incomplete notes.) Taking iPad or iPhone photographs of other people's notes may be useful sometimes.
- Give him time in class and in discussions to formulate his ideas and answers. His thinking may be excellent, but this is a child who may take longer than expected to pull his ideas together into words.
- Remember that homework and assignments will take more of his time than for most pupils, and discuss this with him and his parents.
- Make sure all of his teachers are aware of the situation.

Finding out more

Useful websites

www.dyslexia-information.com/what_is_dyslexia.htm considers processing speed in the wider context of dyslexia.

www.nhs.uk/conditions/dyslexia/Pages/Introduction.aspx provides an overview from the medical perspective.

www.bdadyslexia.org.uk provides information on all aspects of dyslexia, including processing speed difficulties.

www.scilearnglobal.com/ is the site for the Scientific Learning Corporation and the *Fast ForWord* programme.

www.patoss-dyslexia.org/Handwriting speedtest.html is a useful assessment for speed of writing, and the Patoss website provides as well a wealth of other information for teachers.

Books and articles

Most texts that consider processing speed do so in the wider context of dyslexic difficulties – for example:

Ott, P. (2006) *Teaching Children with Dyslexia: A Practical Guide* (Routledge) – practical advice and information for teachers and assistants teaching dyslexic children.

Reid, G. (4th edition 2009) *Dyslexia: A Practitioner's Handbook* (Wiley-Blackwell) – provides an up-to-date and comprehensive overview of the area of dyslexia and specific learning difficulties. Also contains specific chapters on reading, spelling and writing, as well as learning styles and study skills.

Reid, G. (2nd edition 2011) *Dyslexia: A Complete Guide for Parents and those who help them* (Wiley) – provides information on the role parents can play in supporting their dyslexic child.

3.2 How do I respond to and support Working Memory Difficulties?

There may be some mileage in trying to address the underlying weaknesses directly and to train these skills, and certainly performance in the training tasks themselves will often improve satisfyingly. It's less certain that the skill improvements will transfer to everyday learning tasks – but it's still often well worth trying.

Addressing underlying causes and remediating the difficulty

A web search will reveal very many commercial memory training packages – for example, www.masteringmemory.co.uk has some useful training programmes for visual memory, for children and for adults. Many of these target a range of cognitive and perceptual skills simultaneously, and may well be worth considering. But there are too many to comment upon individually here.

- www.york.ac.uk/res/wml – York University's Centre for Working Memory and Learning provides a lot of excellent information and advice about working memory difficulties.
- www.tracyalloway.com – Tracy Alloway's *Jungle* memory package for training working memory emphasises visual working memory.
- http://advancedbrain.com/products market some well-used and valued auditory training programmes – for example, *The Listening Programme* and *BrainBuilder*.
- *Cogmed* computerised, cognitive exercises for different age groups to assist those who have issues relating to short-term memory – see the demo for one age group on YouTube – *Cogmed: Cogmed RM Demonstration*.

Compensating and supporting strategies

- Break down tasks and instructions into small steps – he may find it hard to keep the whole picture in mind.
- Structure and planning: use of headings and sub-headings helps to provide a structure for oral as well as written responses.
- Understanding and following a sequence of instructions can be disproportionately difficult – give instructions one at a time, and offer to repeat information.
- 'Multi-tasking' will be difficult – especially, listening and writing at the same time can be very hard; please allow for this.
- Even activities such as copying from a page or the board can require additional time, as this activity can place a burden on short-term memory and working memory, as the transfer of information may have to be completed in more steps.
- Allow plenty of time for mental operations – especially such things as mental maths, where there is an enormous working memory load – and encourage the use of a jotting pad/scratch pad to help retain information temporarily during mental operations.

◆ There may be problems with learning sight vocabulary, and in modern languages unfamiliar letter strings and written accents may be a challenge – allow for this.

◆ Allow time for answers to oral questions – remember that he does not find it easy to marshal and organise his thoughts.

◆ Allow for short breaks between tasks to allow him to rest.

◆ The *over*-learning which is often necessary for pupils with working memory difficulties means that the learning processing can be more time-consuming: he will need to work for longer on the same task than some other pupils.

◆ Have an agreed format for a personal homework diary. He needs to be able to locate information readily from his diary. An electronic personal organiser can store vast amounts of data and can be synchronised with laptop and desktop computers. Used regularly, this can be extremely beneficial for the older pupil with memory difficulties.

◆ Make sure all of his teachers are aware of the situation.

Finding out more

Useful websites

Baddely, A. D. (2004) *Your Memory: a user's guide* (Edition IV, Carlton) – provides authoritative and in-depth background to all aspects of memory.

Gathercole, S. & Alloway, T. (2008) *Working Memory and Learning: a practical guide for teachers* (Paul Chapman) – a practical and informative book that combines theory with practice.

Hill, M. & Hill, K. (2008) *Auditory Memory Skills* (LDA) – a range of activities that aim to develop auditory memory skills.

Note: a web search will reveal a large number of memory training books aimed at an adult market – for example, Alloway, T. (2010) *Training your Brain for dummies* (Wiley) offers valuable activities and tips aimed at the whole age range, and many of these will work for school-age children – but there are too many to comment upon individually here.

3.3 How do I respond to and support Spelling Difficulties?

Good spelling is something that we all, teachers and parents, seem to value highly. But arguably we're locked into the past with this, when it did matter. Nowadays, significant pieces of writing are seldom done with pen and paper in the workplace, nor in the exam hall if there is a genuine specific barrier to learning that prevents automatic spelling. Keep this in mind when deciding how to respond to spelling difficulties!

Addressing underlying causes

There is nothing to address here that is *specific* to spelling: any underlying causes that may be worth addressing will be subsumed into other strands of difficulty – auditory processing, visual stress, nutritional factors, etc.

Remediating the difficulty

This is certainly worth working on with younger learners – the more you practise any skill, the better you may become at it, and **over-learning** is a central part of responding to all dyslexic-type difficulties: only with a great deal of extra practice will the skill become automatic. But bear in mind the caution above: this is a classic case of quite rapidly diminishing returns. At some point, more spelling practice simply ceases to be a good use of time, and it's better instead to compensate for the weakness by turning to laptop with spellcheck.

How best to provide this over-learning? Software packages such as *Wordshark* now allow masses of extra practice and over-learning in a way that is game-based and fun – see below for this and others.

Compensating and supporting strategies

- Don't make an issue of poor spelling – it is likely that his spelling may remain weak and sometimes apparently careless despite his best efforts. Agree on a modest number of target spelling skills, and focus on these only when you're marking his work.
- Encourage him to get his ideas onto paper without worrying about spelling. If he's worrying about spelling, the much more important skills of developing and conveying ideas and information will stagnate. This may seem hard to begin with for some pupils, since accuracy is stressed so much – but try to make him realise that sometimes he is allowed to be a bit different, and that getting his ideas onto paper is much more important than the spelling.
- Encourage the use of an electronic spellcheck if he seems to find it helpful – but some people don't like them.
- Allow him to explore using a scribe on occasions, so that he can experience the pleasure of getting his ideas onto paper without having to worry about writing and spelling. (Anyone can do this scribing – parents, other pupils, classroom assistants, or other volunteers. Use every source of help that can be found.).

◆ Encourage the development of keyboard skills. A computer with spellcheck is vital for anyone with any writing difficulties, but also it's an invaluable lifeskill for *all* learners.

◆ Consider the use of voice recognition software, once it becomes more robust and user-friendly. (At the time of writing, it does not seem to be a realistic option for most school-age learners with significant literacy difficulties.)

◆ Make sure all of his teachers are aware of the situation.

Finding out more

Useful websites

www.crossboweducation.com – focuses mainly upon reading development, but includes useful spelling games and activities.

www.franklin-uk.co.uk – Franklin *Spellmasters* have developed a range of electronic dictionaries to help master spelling difficulties.
Language master – phonetically spells correctly over 130,000 words and has a built-in grammar guide covering 70 topics.

www.texthelp.com – TextHelp Systems produce excellent and powerful software which can assist in the writing of essays and with grammar and spelling, including *Read & Write Gold*.

www.wordshark.com – *Wordshark* is an enormously rich software package that develops in a very structured and sequential way, by means of very varied games. People of all ages enjoy it.

www.wordwasp.com – *Wordwasp* (Word Articulation Spelling and Pronunciation) is a spelling programme, by Harry Cowling, 'designed for the kitchen table ... for use at home and at school.' It is the spelling equivalent of the very successful *Toe-by-Toe* reading programme.

www.spelling.hemscott.net – valuable practical advice and information for parents, teachers, and adults who find spelling hard, with free worksheets, games, quizzes and puzzles.

www.ttrs.co.uk – a typing course that simultaneously develops reading and spelling, based on the *Alpha to Omega* dyslexia programme.

www.penfriend.biz – provides an excellent word-prediction tool and also has an onscreen keyboard specifically intended for pupils with dyslexia and writing difficulties.

Books and articles

Hornsby, B., Shear, F. & Pool, J. (6th edition, 2006) *Alpha to Omega Pack: Teacher's Handbook and Student's Book* (Heinemann) – a very well tried and comprehensive programme for dyslexic children, that teaches and rehearses all aspects of reading, spelling and correct writing.

Moseley, D. (2009) *ACE Spelling Dictionary* (LDA) – not really a dictionary at all, more an aid to finding spellings – very effective and popular.

Schonell, F. (2000) *The Essential Spelling List* (Nelson Thornes) – lists the 3000 words most commonly used by children in their writing.

3.4 How do I respond to and support Reading Difficulties?

Reading is the most important single literacy skill by far – it's worth working away at developing it in every way possible. Unlike spelling difficulties, which can easily be avoided by strategies such as laptops with spellcheck, we all need to develop our reading ability to its limit.

Addressing underlying causes

As for spelling, there is arguably nothing to address here that is specific to reading: any underlying causes that may be worth addressing will be subsumed into other strands of difficulty – auditory processing, visual stress, nutritional factors, working memory, movement and coordination, etc.

Remediating the difficulty

Look for and pursue every possible way of continuing to work on this. Here are a few effective ones – but there will be so very many others, some of which you will already be familiar with. Just **don't ever give up on it** – reading is arguably the only literacy skill that really matters....

◆ Provide just as much in-school learning support as is possible – reading difficulties are certainly the highest priority by far in deciding how best to allocate scarce support resources.

◆ The *Toe-by-Toe* reading programme focuses upon the underlying mechanics of reading and does not require any specialist training – parents, siblings, peers, neighbours, any of them can work the programme. It's a very good way of working up core decoding skills in a way that complements what you're doing in school (see www.toe-by-toe.co.uk).

◆ Paired reading – this is where parents, relatives, friends or peers read *along with* the child, rather than *listening* to him reading. It can be done in lots of different ways – but the core idea is that the child reads aloud and the partner supplies the word just as soon as there's any hesitation. This lets him keep track of what the text is all about, instead of continuously losing the thread while he puzzles out how to decode the difficult words. The partner can pause and talk about the story and help develop comprehension skills, or focus on decoding skills, just whenever it seems useful to do so. If you want to find out more about how to do it, just Google it – YouTube has some good demonstrations.

Compensating and supporting strategies

◆ Reading aloud in front of others may be difficult and embarrassing. Obviously, it may be necessary in such settings as reading groups, but keep it in mind for other occasions.

◆ Reading aloud and understanding at the same time might be hard – he may be one of the many who can just about cope with one or the other, but simply doesn't have enough attentional resource to do both at once.

- When it makes sense to do so, read things to him or get someone else to, so that reading difficulties don't get in the way of effective learning. Seating him with a helpful peer who's a good reader is often a good idea.
- Do not expect extended and unsupported reading – arrange in advance for important texts to be recorded (a parent or other volunteers can help with this).
- Encourage as much use as possible of 'talking books', as well as reading aloud to younger children. Getting them used to the world of books and literary language is as important for non-readers as for readers – maybe more so. A library may have a supply of audio texts, and there is an increasing range of audio and digital resources available.
- Make requests to examination boards as appropriate for:
  - readers
  - use of ICT
- Make sure all his teachers know of his difficulty, and allow for it in every possible way.

Finding out more

Useful websites

www.bdadyslexia.org.uk – the site of the British Dyslexia Association, offering a wide range of information about all aspects of literacy difficulties.

www.dyslexiaaction.org.uk – previously known as the Dyslexia Institute, and providing information about dyslexia services, provision and assessment.

www.beingdyslexic.co.uk – provides a lot of background information about being dyslexic.

www.dyslexia.com – useful guidance for both teachers and parents.

www.dyslexia.uk.com – a knowledge site providing information and guidance on all topics relating to dyslexia.

www.fifepeerlearning.org – explains and supports ways in which parents, friends or peers can help develop reading through paired reading.

www.listening-books.org.uk – provides an audiobook library service across UK. Listening to books is an enormously important way of developing the language experience of poor readers.

www.lovereading4kids.co.uk – an on-line bookshop with a very wide range of children's books at all levels of readability.

www.calibre.org.uk – a free lending library for those with a recognised disability, including dyslexics if unable to access printed text themselves.

Books and articles

Hornsby, B., Shear, F. & Pool, J. (6th edition, 2006) *Alpha to Omega Pack: Teacher's Handbook and Student's Book* (Heinemann) – a very well tried and comprehensive programme for dyslexic children, that teaches and rehearses all aspects of reading, spelling and correct writing.

Reid, G. (2nd edition, 2011) *Dyslexia: A Complete Guide for Parents and those who help them* (Wiley) – provides information on the role parents can play in supporting their dyslexic child.

3.5 How do I respond to and support Dyscalculia?

Dyscalculic people find aspects of maths and number baffling and frustrating. He just won't be able to do things that other children seem to manage *easily* – and his teachers are going to be as baffled and frustrated as he is.

It will specially affect learning tables, and remembering basic number facts and bonds – for example, most children will 'know' the answer to 7+3, but the dyscalculic child may have to calculate it afresh each time. This gets in the way of other maths learning – the concepts and ideas – which he may well be able to manage.

Don't let the number and mental arithmetic barriers get in the way – intelligent use of number and table squares and calculators can be enormously helpful, and free him up to tackle the *real* mathematical thinking.

Addressing underlying causes

Weak **working memory** can be one of the barriers that cause number difficulties, and it may be worth suggesting his family look at websites like www.york.ac.uk/res/wml, which provides a lot of background information and advice about working memory difficulties (arguably some of these skills are best progressed at home, and it's not realistic for schools to try to work on them).

Remediating the difficulty

Developing fluent and automatic access to number facts is well worth working on – until, that is, it becomes apparent that the point of diminishing returns has obviously been reached, and the horse being flogged is just not improving its performance as a result of the flogging. For most dyscalculic children, this is likely to be before transfer to secondary.

Working on all such areas of weakness involves **over-learning** – for any skills that aren't becoming automatic, masses of extra practice is the only way to get there. *Numbershark* (see below) is one way of doing this relatively painlessly through enjoyable on-screen practice, and can be recommended for use at home or school.

Less painless and more costly to the family, but sometimes very effective, are out-of-school tuition schemes such as Kumon Maths (see below). This gives highly structured and very intensive practice of number skills.

Compensating and supporting strategies

- Do not expect competent recall of number facts or tables – these will be hard.
- Encourage/allow use of a number or table square or calculator whenever possible.
- Use concrete rather than abstract examples to illustrate a problem.
- If you can, allow the use of concrete/physical aids to assist in working out calculations.
- Allow more time for maths problems.

◆ Break problems down into several steps, and allow time for checking and monitoring the progress throughout these steps.

◆ Encourage him to talk through the 'working' to a problem – this can provide the opportunity for suggesting more efficient strategies.

◆ The technical language of maths may be a difficulty – he may understand the general meaning of words such as *difference, evaluate, odd, mean* and *product*, but stumble over their quite different meanings in the context of mathematics.

◆ Ensure that his teachers know about the difficulty if it applies to their subject – for example, he may have a natural and intuitive grasp of physics, and it would be a pity if this were blocked by taking ages each time to work out 9×7, say.

◆ Consider requests to examination boards for use of a calculator, if the examination board allows this.

Finding out more

Useful websites

http://uk.ixl.com – an online Maths practice resource.

www.wordshark.co.uk/numbershark.html – a rich and extensive software package for developing number skills.

www.kumon.com – the Kumon Maths scheme provides out-of-school tuition which allows structured and intensive practice of number skills.

www.ldonline.org/indepth/math – articles, links and resources.

www.dyscalculia.me.uk – resources and information relating to dyscalculia.

www.york.ac.uk/res/wml – background information about working memory

Books and articles

Chinn, S. (2007) *Dealing with Dyscalculia: Sum Hope* (Souvenir Press) – Steve Chinn clearly explains the basic principles of mathematics, how they can be used in various situations to make numbers seem less threatening – and, perhaps for the first time, they will begin to make sense. Numbers are integral to everyday life, from checking the cost of shopping and understanding a train timetable. to calculating the best-value mobile phone deal, and Steve Chinn brings maths into everyday life.

Kay, J. & Yeo, D. (2003) *Dyslexia and Maths* (Fulton) – a useful introduction to the problems faced by pupils with dyslexia difficulties in numeracy and maths.

Peer, L. & Reid, G. (2001) *Dyslexia: Successful Inclusion in the Secondary School* (David Fulton) – specific guidance to secondary school staff on how to support dyslexic students within different subject areas and within the principles and practices of inclusion, including maths difficulties.

Vorderman, C. (2005, 2011) *Maths Made Easy* (Dorling Kindersley) – Carol Vorderman's series of booklets, with notes for parents, for practising maths from pre-school through to Key Stage 2.

3.6 How do I respond to Deficiencies of Essential Fatty Acids?

That dietary factors can affect learning is well known – the book title *They are what you feed them* (below) says it all! But while family diet can be very hard to change, it's very easy to deal with one potentially important part of it.

For some of us, it seems that our uptake of these acids is not optimal, however good our diet, and it can affect all kinds of aspects of our function, from literacy, handwriting and attention through, apparently, to the effectiveness of our immune systems.

There's no advice here for **Remediating the difficulty** or for **Compensating and supporting strategies** – that's covered in the advice for whichever strands may be affected for this learner.

All you can do in school is talk to the home about **Addressing underlying causes**.

These deficiencies can be helped by a course of fatty acid supplements (e.g. *Efalex* and *EyeQ* are both available from UK dispensing chemists at the time of writing).

A course of these dietary supplements can sometimes make a significant difference to some of these conditions, though not always. As long as the stated dose is kept to, however, no harm can come of a trial period.

There is no direct action to be taken by the school, except to encourage the family to undertake a trial, and to monitor for any changes. A double dosage is recommended for 12 weeks to build up the level of these acids in the body, to be sure whether or not there will be improvements, and a trial should continue for at least this length of time.

It may be helpful for the family to discuss the situation with their GP, or a dietician if you have access to one.

Finding out more

Useful websites

www.fabresearch.org – the website for Food and Behaviour Research.

www.durhamtrial.org – details of clinical studies underpinning use of fatty acid supplements.

www.health-train.com/healing-arts – some background information about fatty acids in relation to learning difficulties.

www.healingwithnutrition.com/adisease/add-adhd/learndisability – an American site promoting nutritional responses to learning difficulties.

www.dyslexiaa2z.com/learning_difficulties/dyslexia/dyslexia_fatty_acids – useful information about all aspects of dyslexia, including fatty acid supplementation.

www.ldrc.ca/contents/view_article/204/ – a critical evaluation of the current evidence base for fatty acid supplementation.

Books and articles

Holford, P. & Colson, D. (2006) *Optimum Nutrition for Your Child's Mind* (Piatkus Books) – addressed to parents and packed with easily accessible information, dos and don'ts, charts, case histories, convincing and well-referenced scientific studies, tips and recipes.

Holford, P. & Joyce, F. (reprint 2010) *Smart Food for Smart Kids: Easy Recipes to Boost Your Child's Health and IQ* (Piatkus Books) – a cookbook designed to help parents improve their child's diet.

Portwood, M. (2000) 'Seeing the Signs', in *Special*, Spring 2002 (NASEN).

Richardson, A.J. & Puri, B.K. (2000) 'The potential role of fatty acids in Attention deficit/ hyperactivity disorder (ADHD)', *Prostaglandins Leukotr. Essent. Fatty Acids, 63*, 79–87.

Richardson, A. (reissue 2010) *They Are What You Feed Them: How Food Can Improve Your Child's Behaviour, Learning and Mood* (Harper-Thorson) – this book shows parents how to bring the best choices into their children's everyday diets, and includes simple meal plans and recipes as well as practical guidance on other lifestyle factors.

3.7 How do I respond to and support Phonological Difficulties?

These are difficulties with recognising, processing and organising the underlying sounds that we combine to make up the words we use. They apply directly to the spoken word, but indirectly affect the ability to read and spell, and can be a major contributory factor to dyslexic difficulties.

Addressing underlying causes

If there are real difficulties in separating out, making and manipulating speech sounds, then referral to a speech and language therapist is the best way forward.

Remediating the difficulty

www.idealcurriculum.com/phonological-awareness.html provides an invaluable overview of phonological awareness and how to develop it in children. Advice tends to be aimed at younger learners, since this is when these skills are usually mastered – but the approaches can be adapted for older children

◆ Early literacy programmes such as *Jolly Phonics* provide embracing multisensory support to the acquisition of phonological skills, and can be very effective: www.jollylearning.co.uk.
◆ When moving beyond *making* the sounds to *linking* them to letters and words, seeing the word or combination of letters as well as hearing them is important – this should be done at the same time.
◆ Literacy tuition and learning support should focus upon phonic skills, rather than whole words, to begin with.
◆ When moving on beyond phonemes and units of sound, don't just focus on single words – phonic skills are learned in context, using text passages as well as isolated words.
◆ Try to avoid long lists of words which illustrate phonic structures – a few will suffice.
◆ Use colour-coding and marks to indicate short or long sounds.
◆ Make 'word slides' from cardboard and allow him to experiment with different onsets and rime combinations to make different words.
◆ The *Toe-by-Toe* programme is not aimed specifically at phonological difficulties – but working through it at home will certainly develop these skills, as well as decoding skills. See www.toe-by-toe.co.uk.
◆ The *Phonological Awareness Training* programme teaches children to read, spell and write phonically regular single-syllable words by making analogies. There are no lists of words to remember, no spellings to learn. See www.ucl.ac.uk/educational-psychology/cpd/pat.htm.

There are no **compensating and supporting strategies** that are specific to phonological difficulties. The difficulties will be impacting on the child's spelling and reading, so make use of any strategies from these strands that seem useful.

Finding out more

Useful websites

www.dyslexics.org.uk – a highly recommended coverage of things that can be done at home for all aspects of dyslexic difficulties, including phonological factors.

www.members.tripod.com – provides useful background discussion and information.

www.minddisorders.co.uk – offers a rigorous exploration of how phonological disorders and difficulties sit within a wider framework of speech and language disorders.

www.warwick.ac.uk/staff/D.J.Wray/Articles/phonic.html – a useful and easy-to-read summary.

Books and articles

Bayley, R. & Broadbent, L. (2008) *Helping Young Children with Phonological Awareness* (Lawrence Educational Publications) – contains a wealth of ideas for developing sound discrimination, an appreciation of rhythm, rhyme and alliteration and oral segmenting and blending.

Carmichael, S. & Barrs, G. (2008) *Get Ready for Reading: Developing Phonological Awareness* (Scholastic) – a teaching resource which covers the initial sounds of words (28 sounds in total). Each sound is split into three parts with activities for: preparing the ears for reading, preparing the eyes for reading, and exercising the brain for reading. Activities include nursery rhymes, songs, identifying objects with the sound, listening games and specific physical activities to help stimulate the brain.

Scott, V. (2009) *Phonemic Awareness: Ready-to-Use Lessons, Activities, and Games* (Corwin Press) – this second edition contains an updated collection of 48 lessons for children in the upper Primary years who have difficulty reading. While the activities are sequenced around particular phonemes or sounds, teachers can reorganise and sequence them according to skills such as identification, blending, rhyming, segmentation, deletion, or manipulation.

Spector, C. (2009) *Sounds Like Fun: Activities for Developing Phonological Awareness* (Brookes Publishing Co).

3.8 How do I respond to and support Auditory Processing Difficulties?

Like phonological processing, auditory processing is part of the foundations of literacy. It refers to how sounds, specially word sounds, are received and processed (as opposed to phonological processing, which refers to how the sounds are organised for articulation).

Addressing underlying causes

As suggested in section 2.8, you can't really address these difficulties in the classroom or school. The same specialist approaches that identify the difficulties are used to address them. Some of them – for example, *The Listening Programme* (www.thelisteningprogram.com) and *Johansen* (www.johansenias.com) – may lend themselves better than others to developing an in-school programme, working with a specialist provider; but on the whole these are programmes to be followed by individuals out of school.

Remediating the difficulty

Fast ForWord (www.scilearnglobal.com) is designed specifically for use in schools, and part of its focus includes speed and effectiveness of processing sound. At the time of writing, it's probably true to say that there has not been extensive uptake in UK, and there do not seem to be obvious in-school techniques for *remediating* auditory processing difficulties. They can, however, be *allowed for* very effectively.

Compensating and supporting strategies

◆ Background noise may be extremely distracting – a seat near the blackboard/whiteboard or front of class may help.
◆ Be ready to repeat things – hearing itself is not a problem, but absorbing and processing the information can be laborious. Some pupils may need simple repetition, while others may need what has been said to be rephrased. Most of all, allow *TIME* for processing before expecting a response.
◆ Don't assume he's understood just because he nods or says *'Yes'* when you ask him if he's understood. Get him to repeat back the main points you have made – not verbatim, but in his own words (this is a great way of aiding learning, whether or not there are any auditory processing difficulties!).
◆ Do not expect immediate answers to oral questions, or assume that because his hand is not up he doesn't know the answer – the right answer may be there, but takes time to be formulated.
◆ Establish eye contact when speaking, and use some gesture to support your words.
◆ Cue him with phrases like *'This is important.'*
◆ Speak slowly and clearly and with comfortable loudness, and vary your tone and rate of speech to keep attention and to emphasise important material.
◆ Allow for some measure of frustration – remember that he may be continuously undergoing a 'tip-of-the-tongue' experience.
◆ Ensure that all his teachers know about the difficulty and understand its implications.

Finding out more

Useful websites

Robyn's Nest Parenting network – www.robynsnest.com/audproc.htm

British Society of Audiology – www.thebsa.org.uk

Books and articles

Bellis, T. J. (2002) *When the Brain can't Hear – Unravelling the Mystery of Auditory Processing Disorder* (Pocket Books).

Peer, L. (2005) *Glue Ear, An essential guide for teachers, parents and health professionals* (Fulton).

3.9 How do I respond to and support Expressive and Receptive Language Disorders?

These are the children who are not that good at processing and organising expressive and/or receptive language. They may have been later starting to talk, and their speech may still be rather unclear, muddled, or hard to decipher. The difficulties may well be linked to strands such as auditory and phonological processing, and they can range across:

- Speech – the speech sounds we produce;
- Grammar – the way we put words together to form phrases and sentences;
- Vocabulary and Semantics – words and their meaning;
- Pragmatics – using language appropriately in different social situations.

Addressing underlying causes of language disorders should be left in the main to speech and language professionals. Schools and teachers are not trained or equipped for this. Recommend referral for speech therapy assessment, if this has not already taken place.

Remediating the difficulty

Strategies for **younger children** and more serious difficulties (some of these are worth passing on to parents to use at home):

- He needs to hear the same word again and again, so repeat words and phrases in different ways, such as 'That's a *fabulous* picture, it's really good, it's *fabulous*!'
- Use repetition and chant, such as repeating poems or songs, especially ones that involve sounds.
- Ask open questions instead of closed ones, so that he has to generate his own words to answer, rather than pick some of yours and repeat them – for example *'What do you want to do next?'* is better than *'Do you want to finish your drawing, or do you want to go out and play?'*
- Model with your own language – use pronouns, prepositions, etc, rather than simplifying too much.
- Use chanting, music, rhythm and rhyme to help build up auditory memory.
- Weave language around everyday tasks, so that he is doing and hearing and using at the same time – talk along with the process of getting dressed, playing with Lego, helping with things, etc.

For older children

- Look for every opportunity to stimulate verbal exchanges and processing, through question and answer, keeping it as simple as is needed to start with, but steadily working up the level of complexity.

Compensating and supporting strategies

- Sit him not too far from the teacher. There are usually a lot of oral instructions in class, so it is important to ensure he doesn't lose track of what is being said. This may happen if he's sitting some distance from the teacher, when background noise also may be more distracting.

◆ Don't expect immediate answers to oral questions, or assume that because his hand is not up, he doesn't know the answer – it may be there, but it may take time to be formulated and articulated. We use words for sharing most of our ideas, in the classroom and out – and words are what this child finds hard.

◆ Try to give immediate verbal and non-verbal reinforcement and prompts when he is speaking.

◆ Allow for some measure of frustration – remember he may be continuously undergoing a 'tip-of-the-tongue' experience.

◆ Be careful not to judge overall levels of ability on the basis of his spoken contributions.

◆ Use visual and spatial prompts and aids to learning if and when possible.

◆ In group work, encourage turn-taking to lead the group – this needs to be carefully monitored, but can be a great opportunity for him to develop these skills.

◆ Ensure that all his teachers know about the difficulty and understand its implications.

Finding out more

Useful websites

Afasic – www.afasic.org.uk – a charity for people with communication difficulties.

Association of Speech and Language Therapists in Independent Practice (ASLTIP) – www.helpwithtalking.com – information/database concerning appropriate local therapists.

I CAN – website: www.ican.org.uk – an educational charity for children with speech and language difficulties, training centre for parents and professionals, and numerous factsheets. The Talking Point aims to provide a one-stop shop for professionals and parents.

www.speechdisorder.co.uk is a very comprehensive site, that includes an enormous amount of useful information, resources and activities.

SpeechteachUK – www.speechteach.co.uk – a speech therapy website for parents and professionals supporting children with speech difficulties. The site contains resources, reviews and discussion.

www.mnsu.edu/comdis/kuster/stutter.html – for comprehensive information, advice and resources for stuttering and fluency disorders.

www.kidshealth.org – deals with all aspects of child health, and includes useful material on speech and language disorders and difficulties.

Books and articles

Monschein, M. (2008) *The 50 Best Games for Speech & Language Development* (50 Best Group Games) (Hinton House Publishers) – fun and easy, tried-and-tested games to help develop language skills in children, including activities for motor and listening skills, sound production, sentence formation and more. These activities can be used either in group settings or adapted for use in one-to-one sessions. Games for developing oral and finger motor skills; games for developing concepts; listening games; games for practising problem sounds; games for promoting sentence construction.

Mountstephen, M. & Hughes, C. (2009) *A Practical Guide to Support Children with Speech and Language Difficulties* (Meeting Special Needs) (Practical Pre-School Books) – includes information on the common areas of concern and possible causes, and then provides ideas and practical solutions to support the child and its parents.

3.10 How do I respond to and support Meares–Irlen Syndrome?

Probably most of us are aware of visual discomfort from the pattern on the page or glare at some time or another – but for a few, it's pronounced enough to make reading uncomfortable, even nauseous, and cause real literacy difficulties.

Addressing underlying causes

You can explore the effects of tinted overlays (e.g. from www.crossboweducation.com) – but probably underlying causes are best addressed by an optometrist: the *Visual Stress Assessment Pack* from Crossbow Education includes a 'Find Your Local Visual Stress Specialist' facility.

Remediating the difficulty isn't really an option – practice isn't going to make things better.

Compensating and supporting strategies

◆ Copy text onto photo-enlarged and/or tinted paper – this may not be practicable in everyday classwork, but is especially important for tests and assessments.
◆ Encourage the use of a marker while reading, and a relatively slow pace of reading.
◆ Resources such as the *Visual Tracking Magnifier* can be placed over text and can help those who suffer from pattern glare and fixation problems. The magnifier is a high-powered magnifying glass with a central viewing strip about 7 cm wide. The *VTM Line Reader* is also available and this has shaded areas to mask pattern glare. Both are available from Ian Jordan at Desktop Publications www.desktoppublications.co.uk.
◆ Ensure the lighting is adequate – pupils with visual difficulties will need good lighting, but not glare or fluorescent lights. Natural lighting is best.

Finding out more

Useful websites

www.childrensvision.com – provides a wealth of excellent and accessible information about the experience of visual difficulties, and how they may affect reading, as does www.children-special-needs.org/vision therapy.

www.crossboweducation.com – markets a range of tools for readers affected by visual stress.

www.ioo.org.uk – the website of the Institute of Optometry, includes a useful section about visual aspects of dyslexia.

www.vision3d.com – for useful information on visual health and visual therapies.

www.colour2c.co.uk – the site of a north of England service for Meares–Irlen syndrome.

www.ioo.org.uk – website for the Institute of Optometry.

Books and articles

Evans, B. (2002) *Dyslexia and Vision* (Whurr) – provides information for parents and professionals in relation to visual factors and dyslexia. It also offers an evidence-based review of the literature for eyecare professionals.

Jordan, I. (2002) *Visual Dyslexia: Signs, Symptoms and Assessment* (Desktop Publications) – an accessible guide to visual factors that may affect reading.

Wilkins, A. (2003) *Reading Through Colour* (Wiley-Blackwell) – tells the development of the use of coloured overlays and tinted glasses to assist pupils with reading difficulty.

3.11 How do I respond to and support Visual Stress and Ocular Control issues?

These are difficulties stemming from poor muscular control of eye movement. As with Meares-Irlen Syndrome, **Addressing underlying causes** is best left to an appropriate health professional – usually an optometrist or orthoptist – and the *Visual Stress Assessment Pack* from Crossbow Education includes a 'Find Your Local Visual Stress Specialist' facility.

Remediating the difficulty

Visual specialists are best placed to remediate the difficulty, as well as pinning down the underlying causes – but there are lots of exercises that can be undertaken at home or school, and an excellent source for these is www.eyecanlearn.com (see below).

Compensating and supporting strategies

◆ Give him time to read, encourage a relatively slow pace of reading, and remember he will tire easily.
◆ Provide photo-enlarged text – this may not be practicable for all everyday classwork, but it is specially important for tests and assessments.
◆ Encourage the use of a marker while reading.
◆ Resources like the *Visual Tracking Magnifier* can be placed over text, and can help a lot with eye tracking and fixation – e.g. from www.desktoppublications.co.uk.
◆ Make sure all his teachers know about this problem.
◆ Where appropriate, make requests to exam boards for enlarged-print exam papers.
◆ Make classroom lighting as good as possible, but try to avoid glare or fluorescent lights. Good natural light is best, so maybe a window seat.

Finding out more

Useful websites

www.childrensvision.com gives a lot of excellent and accessible information about the experience of visual tracking difficulties, and how they affect reading, as does www.children-special-needs.org.

www.eyecanlearn.com has a wide range of free, on-screen, visual training exercises.

www.ioo.org.uk is the website of the Institute of Optometry, and has a useful section on the visual aspects of dyslexia.

Books and articles

Evans, B. (2002) *Dyslexia and Vision* (Whurr) provides information for parents and professionals about visual factors and dyslexia.

Jordan, I. (2002) *Visual Dyslexia: Signs, Symptoms and Assessment* (Desktop Publications) – an accessible guide to visual factors that can affect reading and learning.

3.12 How do I respond to and support Dysgraphia?

Dysgraphia refers to poor handwriting and page layout, often combined with spelling difficulties. Because spelling difficulties are dealt with as a separate strand in this book, the suggestions here are for problems specifically with handwriting and page layout.

Addressing underlying causes probably isn't all that meaningful when considering just dysgraphic difficulties in isolation – but some of the approaches discussed in section 3.13, for addressing the possible causes of coordination difficulties, may be worth considering if the handwriting problem is part of a wider range of related difficulties. But there are some activities that may help with underlying causes, such as:

- Encourage 'crossing the midline' activities – e.g. simple juggling, even with just one ball from hand to hand.
- Swimming can be helpful too – as will be most sports, as long as they do not put too much emphasis on competition, and demotivate.

Remediating the difficulty

- Provide as much handwriting practice as seems worthwhile. This is important for younger children – but keep in mind that the learner with a real dysgraphic difficulty will start using a computer for writing at some point, so stay alert for the point of diminishing returns (arguably quite early for lots of pupils).
- Encourage him to verbalise the nature and direction of strokes while practising the shape of individual letters.
- Emphasise the 'Four S's' when discussing handwriting: **S**lope, **S**ize, **S**pacing, **S**itting on the line.
- www.thrass.com is a popular and well-tried approach for teaching handwriting, reading and spelling skills, and involves pre-writing skills such as bead threading, shape and pattern copying, tracing, colouring in, and writing letters in sand.

Compensating and supporting strategies

- Writing can be tiring – allow breaks, and keep the task length manageable.
- Don't use plain paper – lines and squares help organise the page, and double spacing improves legibility.
- A sloping board can be helpful as a writing surface – or a lever-arch folder may do just as well.
- For younger children, encourage the use of a triangular pencil grip.
- Encourage redrafting – sometimes it's good to use a double page with the left side for first draft, and the right side for redrafting.
- Older pupils might find it hard to make legible and usable notes – either provide them, or arrange for him to photocopy a friend's, or perhaps use photos taken with an iPad or iPhone.
- Develop his use of a computer for all of his extended writing – in the rest of his life, paper and pen is going to be yesterday's technology.

◆ Encourage the use of a scribe if it seems helpful – either occasionally, just to let him enjoy the buzz of getting his ideas onto paper (and this can be a good way to take the pain out of some homework tasks), or as a longer-term option, if using a computer isn't going to resolve all the writing difficulties.

◆ Consider requests to exam boards such as for use of ICT, scribes, voice recorder, transcription.

Finding out more

Useful websites

www.dyslexiaa2z.com has a wealth of advice, approaches, activities and responses for all aspects of dysgraphia.

www.inpp.org.uk approaches such difficulties from a particular theoretical standpoint, that of retained primitive reflexes.

www.nha-handwriting.org.uk – a charity dedicated to supporting and improving handwriting difficulties.

Books and articles

Addy, L. (2004) *Speed Up! A kinaesthetic programme to develop fluent handwriting* (LDA) – aimed at 8–13 year olds.

Bennett, J. (2007) *The Handwriting Pocketbook* (Teachers Pocketbooks).

Cavey, D. (2003) *Dysgraphia: Why Johnny Can't Write: A handbook for teachers and parents* (Pro Ed).

3.13 How do I respond to and support Movement, Balance, Coordination and Planning Difficulties?

These kinds of difficulties are very common, to a greater or lesser degree, and are often a strand in other difficulties, such as processing speed, literacy difficulties, language difficulties and, quite often, social and emotional problems. The difficulty can be surprisingly narrow, but still constitute a significant barrier – for example, a pupil may be skilled and talented in some sports, but still disorganised and clumsy in other areas.

Addressing underlying causes and **Remediating the difficulty** tend to overlap for these children.

◆ Programmes of physical exercises are often very helpful, and many schools have some kind of movement programme for such children. Explore this option in-school.

◆ If the problems are significant, seek assessment/input from an occupational therapist.

◆ Explore some of the established therapy programmes for such pupils – e.g. assessment for developmental delays/coordination difficulties, with a possible subsequent therapy programme from INPP (see www.inpp.org.uk).

◆ www.dystalk.com/topics/2-dyspraxia has excellent advice on how best to help.

◆ For younger children, suggest families do as many of these as possible:

For vestibular integration (aspects of balance):
  Swinging – swings, hammocks, tyres from trees
  Walk on unstable surfaces
  Spinning – merry-go-rounds, swivel chairs
  Sliding down slides every which way – sitting, lying, forwards, backwards.....
  Swimming, horse riding
  Balancing on a big ball

For proprioceptive integration (awareness of body position):
  Housework – carrying things, pushing the vacuum cleaner, digging and gardening
  Pushing and pulling barrows, prams, stroller, wagons
  Pillow diving and burrowing onto, into and through piles of pillows, cushions and beanbags
  Playing catch, using a big ball or a cushion or pillow
  Helping in the kitchen – pouring, carrying, mixing

For fine motor skills:
  Blocks, games, Lego, puzzles, jigsaws
  Drawing, painting, colouring, any kind of arts and crafts
  Playdough/Plasticine modelling

◆ Encourage movement training and games like 'Simon Says' with unfamiliar movements, following directions, practising left/right distinctions, etc.

◆ Encourage 'crossing the midline' activities, even just juggling with one ball hand to hand.

◆ Encourage as many games and activities that need fine or gross motor skills, and hand/eye coordination – but keep them light, fun and non-competitive!

◆ Look for ways to make PE lessons as accessible and fun as possible – he's going to look for ways to avoid them if he keeps failing, and he needs these activities.

Compensating and supporting strategies

◆ Multi-tasking is likely to be hard – for example, listening effectively and making notes at the same time – so allow for this.

◆ He's probably having to work disproportionately hard to achieve at the level he is achieving, and will get very tired. He may be a model pupil in school, and take it out on his family at home, causing a lot of distress. Allow for this, and help his family understand what is happening.

◆ Allow lots of time for tasks – he may have to think them out afresh each time he does them: automaticity can take a long time for such children, and things that seem easy to others can take undue effort and attention.

◆ He's likely to be disorganised and chaotic – losing things, forgetting tasks. Help in every way you can – liaise with home over books and equipment needed, check his schoolbag, advise on ways of organising his work, notes, etc.

◆ Cognitive planning can be as hard as physical planning, and techniques such as mindmapping can help. The *Inspirations* package is a very powerful way of setting out and organising ideas – see www.taglearning.com.

Finding out more

Useful websites

www.dyspraxiafoundation.org.uk provides comprehensive information, advice and support for parents and professionals.

www.inpp.org.uk considers dyspraxia-related difficulties from the perspective of retained primitive reflexes, as well as providing movement therapy to address/mitigate the underlying causes.

www.happypuzzle.co.uk/ markets an enormously wide range of resources and activities to develop coordination skills.

www.dystalk.com/talks/56-what-is-dyspraxia-dcd is the website of the Dyscovery Centre in Cardiff, and includes a lot of valuable information.

Books and articles

Addy, L. & Barnes, R. (2003) *How to Understand and Support Children with Dyspraxia* (LDA) – aimed at teachers, assistants and therapists, and offering a wide range of ideas and strategies.

Drew, S. & Atter, E. (2008) *Can't Play, Won't Play: Simply Sizzling Ideas to Get the Ball Rolling for Children with Dyspraxia* (Kingsley) – practical information and tips to help children with DCD to access and enjoy the kinds of activities that other children take for granted.

Lee, M. & Portwood, M. (2004) *Coordination Difficulties: Referral, Assessment and Treatment: Practical Ways Forward* (Fulton) – the action plans in this book will allow you to respond in an immediate and structured way to such difficulties.

3.14 How do I respond to and support Attention Deficit Disorder?

The ADD pupil often seems to be downright lazy – but probably it is due to factors entirely beyond his control, so responding to him as someone who just can't be bothered is going to do more harm than good. As well as being dreamy and inattentive, he's likely to seem sometimes passive and often disorganised.

Addressing underlying causes

Fatty acid supplements may help (e.g. *Eye-Q, Efalex, MorEpa*); and if the problem seems to be deep-seated, and the primary barrier to his learning, then medical referral via his GP may be worth suggesting – medication is not something to be undertaken lightly, but in some cases it may be worth at least exploring.

Remediating the difficulty and **Compensating and supporting strategies** tend rather to run together for the ADD pupil:

- Punishments won't usually establish the desired behaviour – but reinforcing desired behaviours will help.
- Talk with him about the issues – then, as situations seem to be emerging, quietly and explicitly point out what is happening and its likely consequences.
- Stay in the closest possible touch with his parents/carers – they need to be completely in the loop, especially as ADD pupils often have completely unrealistic ideas about how well they are coping.
- Seating – discuss with him where he is most likely to work well and stay on task (and if possible away from other pupils who tend to be easily distracted).
- Minimise potential distractions around his part of the classroom.
- Remember that ADD pupils attend to what is most stimulating to them at that moment, so be as simple and attention-grabbing as you can – a slow monotone or a long preamble will be a definite switch-off.
- Alert his attention with markers such as 'This bit's really important.'
- Consider target-setting and reward schemes, with short-term and attainable targets to increase on-task time.
- Giving him an egg-timer and allowing 'move-about' breaks after agreed periods of sustained and silent work can be helpful.
- Set pieces of work as a sequence of small and achievable chunks, and present information in the same way.
- Be endlessly calm and patient in recalling his wandering attention – eye contact, desk taps, or any other agreed signal.
- Keep plugging away at organisation techniques which are based on *writing it down somewhere* – he's not going to be able to rely on his memory.
- Help him organise his work – e.g. he should: write the date on each piece of paper as soon as he gets it; have a sectioned working file in his schoolbag, and transfer papers into separate files for each area when he gets home.
- Agree with him and his family how best to monitor and check these arrangements.
- Consider a hand-held electronic planner for older pupils.

Finding out more

Note: lots of these sources slump together ADD and hyperactivity, so you may need to trawl through and cherry-pick if attention deficit is the main problem.

Useful websites

www.dystalk.com has useful information about all aspects of these difficulties.

www.adders.org has a wide range of resources, tips and information.

www.add.org is one of many useful US sites with a lot of background information and resources.

www.nhs.uk/conditions/Attention-deficit-hyperactivity-disorder/Pages/Introduction.aspx is the NHS site for this condition, and like many other sources it regards ADD as a subtype of ADHD.

Books and articles

Green, C. & Chee, K. (1997) *Understanding ADD – A Parent's Guide to Attention Deficit Disorder* (Vermilion).

Kurtz, L. (2008) *Understanding Controversial Therapies for Children with Autism, Attention Deficit Disorder and other Learning Difficulties: a guide to complementary and alternative therapies* (Jessica Kingsley).

Pentecost, D. (2000) *Parenting the ADD Child – Can't Do, Won't Do?* (Jessica Kingsley).

3.15 How do I respond to and support Hyperactive Difficulties?

Again, there is a lot of overlap in looking at Hyperactivity, as it often presents alongside ADD and/or Impulsivity, so that a lot of the advice and some of the sources are shared in common.

Like the ADD child, this boy is likely to be inattentive, unmotivated and disorganised, but will as well be over-energetic, restless, fidgety. He drives his teachers mad – but, as with other such barriers, he's usually not being naughty or deliberately disruptive: *he just can't help himself*. He's not a 'problem child' – he's a child trying to cope with a problem.

Addressing underlying causes

As for ADD, fatty acid supplements may help to some extent (e.g. *Eye-Q*, *Efalex*, *MorEpa*), and dietary factors may well be worth exploring, with a dietician or independently (e.g. see www.fabresearch.com). If the problem seems to be deep-seated, and the primary barrier to his learning, then medical referral via his GP may be worth suggesting – medication is not something to be undertaken lightly, but in some cases it may be worth at least exploring.

Obviously, decisions about all of these courses of action lie with the family. You can do little more than advise – and remember, when you do so, to have realistic expectations: changing eating behaviours can be very hard.

Remediating the difficulty

◆ Be very aware of what he eats – food additives can have an immediate ill-effect on behaviour for some children.

Apart from this, the best way forward is to develop support strategies that help him manage his own behaviour, at school and at home. Once he's experiencing success in his learning, and it's becoming more intrinsically rewarding, he'll start to find his own ways of remediating the difficulty.

Compensating and supporting strategies

◆ Punishments won't usually establish the desired behaviour – but reinforcing desired behaviours will help.
◆ Talk with him about the issues – then, as situations seem to be emerging, quietly and explicitly point out what is happening and its likely consequences.
◆ Use target setting and rewards – discuss this with him so that he feels part of the process, rather than it being something that is being 'done to him'.
◆ Stay in the closest possible touch with his parents/carers – this is especially important in delivering rewards for good work and targets met.
◆ He will often be a very frustrating pupil to teach – but try to remember that what looks like naughty behaviour probably isn't intended as such – and he

may have a lot of bad habits to unlearn before he can start to cope better with himself.

◆ If possible, seat him among children who do not normally have problems with behaviour or overactivity.

◆ Minimise potential distractions around his part of the classroom.

◆ He *needs* to be active – let him play with something in his hands as long as he doesn't disturb others, and give him jobs to do that let him move around the classroom.

◆ Remember that ADHD pupils attend to what is most stimulating to them at that moment, so be as simple and attention-grabbing as you can – a slow monotone or a long preamble will be a definite switch-off.

◆ Alert his attention with markers such as *'This bit's really important.'*

◆ Remember that for every difficult kid you've succeeded with, each one of them will have felt that *'The thing I like about you best... is that **you** like **me**!'*

◆ Avoid confrontation – offer choice and options.

◆ When meltdown happens (and it will), allow space and time and postpone the discussion you have to have with him.

◆ Don't take difficult behaviours personally – he wants to be like other pupils, and be successful and be liked – it's just that he hasn't yet worked out how to.... He needs all the patient help he can get to start learning how to deal with his problems.

◆ Try to understand – ask yourself **'Why did he do that?'** There's always a reason, even if it's not rational or productive (and usually it isn't!).

◆ Be flexible – **if it's working, go on doing it**; and if it's not, **do something else**. Use the DIRM approach... **D**oes **I**t **R**eally **M**atter? Choose your battles – while we often feel a child has to conform for his own sake, as the essential first step towards helping him, sometimes it's better to let it go, explaining why to him, and explaining that you're still working together towards helping him learn to conform.

◆ Be ready sometimes to **back off** and **walk away**. Come back to the issue when you're both calmer – and explain that the cooling off time is not punishment. He's not *'won'* if he's allowed some soothing activity in the interim: he knows you'll be coming back to it ten minutes down the line....

Finding out more

Useful websites

www.adhdandyou.co.uk has sections for teachers, parents/carers and for health professionals.

www.fabresearch.co.uk explores all aspects of the links between what we eat and how we behave and how we learn.

www.chadd.org is a US site with a lot of suggestions, information and resources aimed at supporting ADHD children.

www.livingwithadhd.co.uk has invaluable information about identification, management and treatment options.

Books and articles

Hoopman, K. (2008) *All Dogs Have ADHD* (Jessica Kingsley) – an absorbing and insightful book that takes a refreshing approach to the joys and challenges of raising a child who is different.

Jackson, J. (2004) *Multi-coloured Mayhem – Parenting the many shades of Adolescents and Children with Autism, Asperger Syndrome and ADHD* (Jessica Kingsley) – a description of family life with children with these difficulties.

Kewley, G. (2010) *Attention Deficit Hyperactivity Disorder: What Can Teachers Do?* (Routledge).

Laver-Bradbury, C., Thompson, M., Weekes, A. & Daley, D. (2010) *Step-by-Step Help for Children with ADHD – a self-help manual for parents* (Jessica Kingsley) – lots of tried and tested ideas for parents and professionals supporting younger children with ADHD.

Rief, S. (2008) *ADD/ADHD Checklist* (Jossey-Bass) – useful background and specific advice for teachers and for parents.

3.16 How do I respond to and support Impulsivity?

Impulsivity is often accompanied by attention problems and hyperactivity issues – but sometimes it does occur on its own. Diet may be worth looking at, and reducing additives in food – maybe suggest getting advice from a dietician.

But these 'rushing and blurting' behaviours will be ***learned*** behaviours, at least in part, and rather than **Addressing underlying causes** or **Remediating the difficulty**, it makes more sense to focus on classroom strategies that will help him ***unlearn*** these behaviours.

Compensating and supporting strategies

- Talk it through with him, to help him understand how it's affecting his work.
- Reward him for *not* being the first with his hand up to answer questions.
- Reward him for *not* being the first to finish a piece of work.
- Break tasks down into small chunks to begin with, so that he can reach agreed targets without having to wait too long for the satisfaction of completing each bit – but talk through with him the need to make the tasks longer, and for him to recognise the achievement of *not* rushing headlong towards the end point.
- Agree targets and rewards for these increasing lengths of tasks.
- Stay in close touch with his family/carers, and agree targets and rewards with them, as well as rewards you can give in school. They can help him unlearn these behaviours in lots of ways – e.g. choosing between getting his pocket money or allowance now, at the usual time, or deferring it a little and getting a little more. This may help him understand that waiting and deferring and reflecting are useful skills, and they are the skills that he is practising.

Finding out more

Again, there is a lot of overlap between impulsivity and hyperactivity, and these sources are shared in common.

Useful websites

www.adhdandyou.co.uk has sections for teachers, parents/carers and for health professionals.

www.fabresearch.co.uk explores all aspects of the links between whar we eat and how we behave and how we learn.

www.chadd.org is a US site with a lot of suggestions, information and resources aimed at supporting ADHD children.

www.livingwithadhd.co.uk has invaluable information about identification, management and treatment options.

Books and articles

Hoopman, K. (2008) *All Dogs Have ADHD* (Jessica Kingsley) – an absorbing and insightful book that takes a refreshing approach to the joys and challenges of raising a child who is different.

Jackson, J. (2004) *Multi-coloured Mayhem – Parenting the many shades of Adolescents and Children with Autism, Asperger Syndrome and ADHD* (Jessica Kingsley) – a description of family life with children with these difficulties.

Kewley, G. (2010) *Attention Deficit Hyperactivity Disorder: What Can Teachers Do?* (Routledge).

Laver-Bradbury, C., Thompson, M., Weekes, A. & Daley, D. (2010) *Step-by-Step Help for Children with ADHD – a self-help manual for parents* (Jessica Kingsley) – lots of tried and tested ideas for parents and professionals supporting younger children with ADHD.

Rief, S. (2008) *ADD/ADHD Checklist* (Jossey-Bass) – useful background and specific advice for teachers and for parents.

3.17 How do I respond to and support Sensory Integration Difficulties and Sensitivities?

These difficulties are often linked to, or mimic, dyspraxic difficulties, ASD, and other developmental difficulties and delays. They are sometimes called *Sensory Modulation Disorders*. They can affect vision, touch, taste, sound, smell, movement and position, and pupils may be over-processing or under-processing. There are no defects in the senses themselves – it's the way the brain is interpreting and analysing them that can cause confusion or intolerable discomfort, or even pain. A person with these difficulties may:

◆ be physically clumsy;
◆ have difficulty learning new movements;
◆ have unusually high or low activity levels;
◆ have poor body awareness;
◆ show extreme over- or under-reactions to some everyday sensations;
◆ be distractible, impulsive or inattentive;
◆ show poor self-care;
◆ have low self-esteem and some social/emotional difficulties.

Their sensory world may fluctuate and range from inert to chaotic, in a way that's hard to understand for others – imagine perhaps you are having to concentrate and work while being surrounded by flashing lights, nauseous smells, sudden loud noises, or being physically jostled and shoved, and you'll maybe have some idea of how it may be for them.

Addressing underlying causes

Suggest that his parents talk with their GP, and consider referral for occupational therapy assessment.

Remediating the difficulty

Parents and carers are probably best placed to watch him and learn what sensory environment is best – observe what arouses him, what calms him, and help him be reflective about it, to talk about it. People who experience these difficulties talk about a wide range of physical experiences that can soothe them, and it's worth talking with his parents/carers about providing experiences like these.

For the **hyposensitive** child, provide extra stimulation:

◆ eating foods with a range of sensory experiences – crackers, apples, celery, carrots, ice cubes, mashed potatoes, dried fruits...;
◆ drinking liquids of varying temperatures or with bubbles;
◆ taking a shower;
◆ jumping or bouncing;
◆ hanging by the hands from a bar.

For the **hypersensitive** child, decreasing hyper responses to sensory stimulation might include:

- sucking on a pacifier, frozen fruit, ice cream, or a boiled sweet;
- back rubbing or cuddling;
- rocking or swaying slowly back and forth;
- taking a bath.

Activities to develop **tactile integration** could include:

- finger drawing – with your finger, draw shapes or letters or numbers to be guessed on his back;
- sandbox searching – hide small objects in a sandbox and have him search for them by touch;
- bathtime – experiment with different textures: sponges, loofahs, flannels, soaps, creams, lotions;
- read books, with or without you, in a rocking chair or bean bag;
- pets – brush a dog, stroke a cat, cuddle a rabbit...;
- human sandwich – lie him down on a mat, while you pretend to spread jam all over him with firm downward strokes, then fold the mat over and press firmly up and down to squish out the excess jam – he will enjoy the deep, soothing pressure of this activity;
- dressing up – have a dressing-up box that has a range of different weights and textures of fabrics.

Compensating and supporting strategies

No two pupils with such issues will have the same needs – and the needs of each one may vary day-by-day. So classroom arrangements have to be based on him talking to you about what he needs. The kinds of things you should talk through are:

- Is there a part of the room where he feels most comfortable?
- Does he feel more comfortable with bright or subdued lighting?
- Are there noises or sounds that affect him badly, or circumstances that make listening specially hard?
- Are there particular parts of the school he's specially uncomfortable in?
- What activities or parts of the school day are specially hard, and why?

Obviously, he needs to understand that there are limits to the accommodations that may be made for him; and that it is *his* responsibility, not just the school's, to find the 'sensory diet' that works best for him. Obviously, too, his family/ carers need to be closely and continuously involved.

- Try to control the physical environment as much as possible, to avoid over- or under-stimulation.
- An 'opt-out' card may be useful, so that he can withdraw to an agreed safe place when he feels overwhelmed or overloaded. A useful target for him would be to reduce the number of times he needs to use it.
- As far as possible, engage his peers in trying to understand and help. He's likely to have driven you and them to distraction on occasions – but they can be remarkably understanding and insightful.

Finding out more

Useful websites

www.comeunity.com/disability/sensoryintegration/carol-kranowitz.html is an interview with the author of the *Out-of-Sync Child* (see below), of particular interest to parents.

www.cot.co.uk – the website of the British Association of Occupational Therapists – College of Occupational Therapists.

www.dyspraxiafoundation.org.uk provides comprehensive information, advice and support for parents and professionals.

www.tsbvi.edu/seehear/fall97/sensory.htm provides a very thorough explanation of these difficulties, and the options available in responding to them.

www.kidsmatters.com.au/sensory-modulation-disorders-smd is another site that explains the difficulties and how to address them.

Books and articles

Biel, L. (2009) *Raising a Sensory Smart Child* (Penguin) – an easy-to-read guide to families about how to understand and respond to sensory issues.

Kranowitz, C. (2005) *The Out-of-Sync Child* (US Imports) – for parents, teachers and therapists, offering understanding of and insight into these difficulties, the ways they can affect everyday life, and how some of the difficulties may be addressed.

3.18 How do I respond to and support Social Awareness and Communicative Disorders ?

These are children who often stand out as difficult, unusual or eccentric, often loners – by choice or otherwise. To some degree, greater or lesser, their difficulties place them on the Asperger's/autistic spectrum. They find it hard to make friends, and to understand how other people are thinking. They don't understand that they are expected to behave in different ways in different circumstances. They may seem very tactless, and take everything very literally. They may have obsessive interests, or be perfectionists. They may have an overactive imaginative/fantasy world, and will often appear rude and arrogant.

Addressing underlying causes

There are a number of programmes and approaches that seek to lessen the impact of these disorders, such as ABA (Applied Behavioural Analysis), TEACCH, speech and language training, occupational therapy and diet-based approaches, and they have in common that they do not set out to 'cure' autism, but rather to respond to it in ways that are optimal for the individual. There are other, more controversial and invasive therapies, including medication, which lie well beyond the scope of the normal school. There are some ways of remediating the difficulties a little, but the core of a child's support should be built around compensating and supporting him in his everyday life while he steadily learns how better to manage for himself.

Remediating the difficulty

◆ For younger children, an adult or older child might act the part of a same-age friend, so that the child can practise social skills, and social behaviour can be modelled, with turn-taking, listening, etc.
◆ 'Social stories' can be a helpful way of learning responses to specific social situations that are likely to be challenging (see the book by Carol Gray, below).
◆ Drama classes can provide a helpful way for him to explore feelings and rehearse social behaviours.

Compensating and supporting strategies

◆ Create a calm, predictable and consistent working environment.
◆ Keep change to a minimum, and give plenty of warning well in advance.
◆ Try to keep his arousal level low, and minimise sensory distractions.
◆ Recognise that 'fun time' and unstructured situations are what he finds hardest.
◆ Never be confrontational with him – it will make things worse.
◆ Make sure he understands exactly what is expected of him.
◆ Use simple and direct language, and address him by name – he won't necessarily recognise that instructions given to the whole class are meant for him too.

- Remember his limited ability to interpret social cues and subtleties of spoken language – he's likely to take situations very literally and at their face value (a nice example: the boy who stated that he couldn't use the escalators on the Underground because the notice said that 'Dogs must be carried', and he didn't have a dog).
- Explore using pictures and visual cues to explain tasks – some ASD children find this much easier.
- Accept that he may have some quite rigid and obsessional behaviours.
- Understand that he may be desperate to avoid some social situations, and allow for it.
- Allow him sometimes to be solitary – he may sometimes feel very threatened by others.
- Encourage and develop his independence and decision-making, but do so slowly and step by step.
- Talk with him about his uniqueness – where the difficulties are very obvious and significant, the Asperger's label can sometimes be very helpful and empowering, and help him understand just *why* he feels different. Luke Jackson's account of his feelings and experiences in *Freaks, Geeks and Asperger's Syndrome* (see below) may be a helpful part of this process.
- Encourage his peer group to understand the situation.
- Encourage him consciously to observe and learn from others' behaviour, and to imitate helpful patterns of behaviour – he won't be doing so instinctively, but will be able to do so consciously more and more effectively as he gets older.
- This is something he needs to understand about himself if he is going to learn to be happy with who he is – there is a telling quote from an autistic child: *'I need help growing **into** this, not **out** of it'.*

Finding out more

Useful websites

www.nas.org.uk is the website of the National Autistic Society – their strap-line, tellingly, is *'Accept Difference…'.*

www.asperger-advice.com – an extremely comprehensive and useful overview.

www.teacch.com – lots of ideas about environmental structure and supporting communication.

Books and articles

Jackson, L. (2002) *Freaks, Geeks and Asperger's Syndrome – a User's Guide to Adolescence* (Jessica Kingsley) – an enormously engaging account from an adolescent boy with AS about every aspect of his daily life, which provides unique insights for parents, teachers and other children.

Boyd, B. (2003) *Parenting a Child with Asperger's Syndrome: 200 tips and strategies* (Jessica Kingsley) – the author is mother to 13-year-old Kenneth, and the book shares all the tips and strategies she has gathered that have helped him.

Frith, U. (2008) *Autism: a very short introduction* (OUP) provides a simple, clear and rigorous summary of the difficulties.

Gray, C. (2010) *The New Social Story Book* (Future Horizons) – how to use this widely used and proven technique.

Griffin, S. & Sandler, D. (2009) *Motivate to Communicate: 300 games and activities for your child with autism* (Jessica Kingsley) – easy to implement games and activities that provide learning opportunities out of everyday situations.

Notbohm, E. & Zysk, V. (2010) *1001 Great Ideas for Teaching and Raising Children with Autism or Asperger's* (Future Horizons) – offers teachers and parents answers to the day-by-day challenges of autism.

Wing, L. (2003) *The Autistic Spectrum: a Guide for Parents and Professionals* (Robinson) – a basic text for professionals, as well as for parents.

Appendix 1

Record Sheet 1: SpLD Assessment Checklist and Outcomes

Pupil name	Date of assessment	Age at assessment	Assessing teacher/staff member

Initial questions **Strands to explore for 'Yes' responses** **Record of outcomes**

Initial questions for Cluster 1 ('phonological dyslexic')

As well as some difficulties with core skills, does s/he...	Yes or No
• Forget or confuse what people say?	
• Show perceptible delays in reaction times – replying to questions; hesitations and pauses?	
• Have difficulty in finding the words s/he wants when talking – i.e. knows what he/she wants to say but has difficulty/delay in putting it into words?	

Reading difficulties
Spelling difficulties
Dyscalculia
Dysgraphia
Phonological difficulties
Auditory processing difficulties
Working memory
Processing speed
Expressive and receptive language disorders
Deficiency in essential fatty acids

Initial questions for Cluster 2 ('visual dyslexic')

As well as some difficulties with core skills, does s/he...	Yes or No
• Seem to have sore eyes?	
• Suffer from headaches or migraines?	
• Seem to depend on a finger or a ruler/marker to stop him/her losing the place too often?	

Reading difficulties
Spelling difficulties
Dyscalculia
Dysgraphia
Visual tracking and ocular control
Meares-Irlen Syndrome
Processing speed
Deficiency in essential fatty acids

Initial questions for Cluster 3 (dyspraxic and coordination issues)

As well as some difficulties with core skills, does s/he...	Yes or No
• Seem particularly untidy and disorganised?	
• Dislike PE and ball games?	
• Seem clumsy and accident-prone?	

Reading difficulties
Spelling difficulties
Dyscalculia
Dysgraphia
Movement, balance and coordination
Processing speed
Deficiency in essential fatty acids

Initial questions for Cluster 4 (attentional and hyperactivity issues)

As well as some difficulties with core skills, does s/he...	Yes or No
• Find it really hard to sit still?	
• Blurt out answers?	
• Lose his/her attention again and again?	

Reading difficulties
Spelling difficulties
Dysgraphia
Impulsivity
Attention deficit disorder
Hyperactivity
Deficiency in essential fatty acids

Initial questions for Cluster 5 (ASD/Asperger's)

As well as some difficulties with core skills, does s/he...	Yes or No
• Hate change and cling to routines?	
• Have no idea about how to make and retain friends?	
• Talk at people, rather than with them, often boring the listener with an obsessive amount of information?	

Reading difficulties
Spelling difficulties
Dysgraphia
ASD/Aspergers
Sensory integration difficulties and sensitivities

Strand of difficulty	Strands to explore	Need identified? Yes/No
Processing Speed difficulties		
Working Memory difficulties		
Movement, Balance, Coordination and Planning difficulties		
Sensory Integration Difficulties and Sensitivities		
Autistic Spectrum Disorders and Asperger's Syndrome.		
Dysgraphia		
Dyscalculia.		
Spelling difficulties		
Reading difficulties		
Phonological difficulties		
Auditory Processing difficulties		
Meares-Irlen syndrome		
Visual Tracking and Ocular Control issues		
Expressive and Receptive Language disorders		
Attention Deficit Disorder		
Hyperactive difficulties		
Impulsivity		
Deficiencies of Essential Fatty Acids		

Record Sheet 2: The 'Yes' responses
Profile arising from record of outcomes

Name				Date	
Strand of difficulty	**Strands where need identified**	**Evidence and/or test scores**		**Strands suggesting possible SEN**	**Level of need: Mild/ Moderate/ Significant**
Processing Speed difficulties				SpLD Dyslexia	
Working Memory difficulties					
Movement, Balance, Coordination and Planning difficulties				SpLD Dyspraxia	
Sensory Integration Difficulties and Sensitivities				SpLD Dyspraxia and/or ASD/ Asperger's	
Autistic Spectrum Disorders/Asperger's Syndrome.				ASD/Asperger's	
Dysgraphia				SpLD Dysgraphia	
Dyscalculia				SpLD Dyscalulia	
Spelling difficulties				SpLD Dyslexia	
Reading difficulties				SpLD Dyslexia	
Phonological difficulties					
Auditory Processing difficulties					
Meares-Irlen syndrome					
Visual Tracking and Ocular Control					
Expressive and Receptive Language disorders				Specific Language Disorders	
Attention Deficit Disorder				ADHD	
Hyperactive difficulties				ADHD	
Impulsivity				ADHD	
Deficiencies of Essential Fatty Acids					

Appendix 2

A completed SpLD Assessment Checklist and Outcomes

Tomas is a ten-year-old boy who has had obvious reading and spelling difficulties – but focusing just on developing these skills isn't making much difference.

Using the **SpLD Assessment Checklist and Outcomes** sheet (see Appendix 1), you worked your way down the left-hand table of **Initial Questions**, and found that you decided **Yes** for **Cluster 1** and **Cluster 3**. It seems Tomas may be a boy with difficulties that are both dyslexic and dyspraxic in nature, with the dyslexic difficulties apparently not being down to any visual processing difficulties.

Looking down the middle column, of **Strands to explore for Yes responses**, you found you could now tick off in the right-hand table all the strands you wanted to explore for Tomas.

Some of these you maybe already knew about, so you didn't need to do any more assessment – for example, you could just write in **Yes** for the **Reading** and **Spelling** strands in the **Needs Confirmed** column of the right-hand table. For others, you did do more assessment and exploration, using the advice and approaches given in Part 2. You found some of the suggested strands *were* important, and others *weren't*; and you showed this by entering **Yes** or **No** in the last column of the table.

At the end, the list of **Yes** responses in that right-hand column summarises all the strands of difficulty you have found for Tomas:

◆ Processing speed
◆ Movement, balance, coordination and planning
◆ Dysgraphia
◆ Spelling difficulties
◆ Reading difficulties, and
◆ Deficiencies in essential fatty acids

This is how it looked:

Record Sheet 1: SpLD Assessment Checklist and Outcomes

Pupil name	Date of assessment	Age at assessment	Assessing teacher/staff member
Tomes Linden	03/04/12	10 years 3 months	Amy wainwright

Initial questions Strands to explore for 'Yes' responses Record of outcomes

Initial questions for Cluster 1 ('phonological dyslexic')

As well as some difficulties with core skills, does s/he...	Yes or No
• Forget or confuse what people say?	Yes
• Show perceptible delays in reaction times – replying to questions; hesitations and pauses?	
• Have difficulty in finding the words s/he wants when talking – i.e. knows what he/she wants to say but has difficulty/delay in putting it into words?	

Reading difficulties
Spelling difficulties
Dyscalculia
Dysgraphia
Phonological difficulties
Auditory processing difficulties
Working memory
Processing speed
Expressive and receptive language disorders
Deficiency in essential fatty acids

Initial questions for Cluster 2 ('visual dyslexic')

As well as some difficulties with core skills, does s/he...	Yes or No
• Seem to have sore eyes?	No
• Suffer from headaches or migraines?	
• Seem to depend on a finger or a ruler/marker to stop him/her losing the place too often?	

Reading difficulties
Spelling difficulties
Dyscalculia
Dysgraphia
Visual tracking and ocular control
Meares-Irlen Syndrome
Processing speed
Deficiency in essential fatty acids

Initial questions for Cluster 3 (dyspraxic and coordination issues)

As well as some difficulties with core skills, does s/he...	Yes or No
• Seem particularly untidy and disorganised?	Yes
• Dislike PE and ball games?	
• Seem clumsy and accident-prone?	

Reading difficulties
Spelling difficulties
Dyscalculia
Dysgraphia
Movement, balance and coordination
Processing speed
Deficiency in essential fatty acids

Initial questions for Cluster 4 (attentional and hyperactivity issues)

As well as some difficulties with core skills, does s/he...	Yes or No
• Find it really hard to sit still?	No
• Blurt out answers?	
• Lose his/her attention again and again?	

Reading difficulties
Spelling difficulties
Dysgraphia
Impulsivity
Attention deficit disorder
Hyperactivity
Deficiency in essential fatty acids

Initial questions for Cluster 5 (ASD/Asperger's)

As well as some difficulties with core skills, does s/he...	Yes or No
• Hate change and cling to routines?	No
• Have no idea about how to make and retain friends?	
• Talk at people, rather than with them, often boring the listener with an obsessive amount of information?	

Reading difficulties
Spelling difficulties
Dysgraphia
ASD/Aspergers
Sensory integration difficulties and sensitivities
Deficiency in essential fatty acids

Strand of difficulty	Strands to explore	Need identified? Yes/No
Processing Speed difficulties	✓	Yes
Working Memory difficulties	✓	No
Movement, Balance, Coordination and Planning difficulties	✓	Yes
Sensory Integration Difficulties and Sensitivities		
Autistic Spectrum Disorders and Asperger's Syndrome.		
Dysgraphia	✓	Yes
Dyscalculia.	✓	No
Spelling difficulties	✓	Yes
Reading difficulties	✓	Yes
Phonological difficulties	✓	No
Auditory Processing difficulties		No
Meares-Irlen syndrome		
Visual Tracking and Ocular Control issues		
Expressive and Receptive Language disorders	✓	No
Attention Deficit Disorder		
Hyperactive difficulties		
Impulsivity		
Deficiencies of Essential Fatty Acids	✓	Yes

Record Sheet 2: The 'Yes' responses
Profile arising from record of outcomes

Name Tomas Linden			Date 03/04/12	
Strand of difficulty	**Strands where need identified**	**Evidence and/or test scores**	**Strands suggesting possible SEN**	**Level of need: Mild/ Moderate/ Significant**
Processing Speed difficulties	Yes	Slightly below average single-word reading speed and 1 min writing on DST; very low PhAB naming Speed	SpLD Dyslexia	Moderate
Working Memory difficulties				
Movement, Balance, Coordination and Planning difficulties	Yes	SNAP balancing task hard, and parental and teacher reports of clumsiness, and poor fine coordination	SpLD Dyspraxia	Moderate
Sensory Integration Difficulties and Sensitivities			SpLD Dyspraxia and/or ASD/Asperger's	
Autistic Spectrum Disorders/Asperger's Syndrome.			ASD/Asperger's	
Dysgraphia	Yes	Poor and slow handwriting, though legible, and found SNAP Figuree copying task very hard.	SpLD Dysgraphia	Moderate
Dyscalculia.			SpLD Dyscalulia	
Spelling difficulties	Yes	Standardised score of 78 on Dyslexia Portfolio Spelling; spelling very erratic and uncertain, and far below the level expected from the high quality of his ideas for writing	SpLD Dyslexia	Significant
Reading difficulties	Yes	Standardised score of 81 on Dyslexia Portfolio single-word reading — though comprehension better, if he has as much time as he needs	SpLD Dyslexia	Significant
Phonological difficulties				
Auditory Processing difficulties				
Meares-Irlen syndrome				
Visual Tracking and Ocular Control				
Expressive and Receptive Language disorders			Specific Language Disorders	

Attention Deficit Disorder			ADHD	
Hyperactive difficulties			ADHD	
Impulsivity			ADHD	
Deficiencies of Essential Fatty Acids	Yes	Parental report suggests a number of allergies, dry skin and dandruff; and parents and Tomas feel that taking supplements helps him concentrate		Mild

Putting all that together to decide what next for Tomas, his difficulties with **Processing Speed** and **Movement, Balance and Coordination** and **Dysgraphia** are all *'moderate'*, and his **Deficiency in Essential Fatty Acids** seems *'mild'*. These are **learning needs** that might be met within the school and supported by local resources – as we did with School Action and School Action Plus – and the advice in Part 3 will point the way.

But the *'Significant'* entries against **Reading** and **Spelling** are clearly suggesting that **Dyslexia** is a very real issue for Tomas, and may well merit being described as an **SEN**, and possibly even merit an **Education, Health and Care Plan.** So consider onward referral and possible assessment by an educational psychologist – this may be the only way Tomas will be able to access the level of support he needs.

Appendix 3

Photocopiable assessment resources

The assessment 'probes' on the following pages are photocopiable resources which have been adapted from the author's computer-aided **Special Needs Assessment Profile for specific learning difficulties (SNAP-SpLD)**. Note that they are intended only for use with pupils aged 5 upto 14, and are not extensively standardised. They offer approximate 'clinical insights' rather than more objective measures, and they do not aim to rank or make fine distinctions between levels of performance – but may still be of real value where other instruments are less easily available.

Where appropriate, refer to the interpretation graphs provided to evaluate the extent of a pupil's difficulty on each task. Performance falling in the 25–50% band is below average and indicates some difficulties; performance in the 'below 25%' band indicates clear difficulties.

Probes *(photocopiable resources)*
Picture Naming
Backward Span
Visual Memory
Vergence and Visual Tracking
Figure Copying
Balancing
Bilateral Integration

Interpretation graphs
Picture Naming
Backward Span
Visual Memory
Figure Copying
Balancing

Picture Naming – Instructions

Equipment required

● Marking sheet   ● Picture sheets 1 & 2   ● Timer

Instructions to be read out to the child

● *I'm going to ask you to look at some pictures and then* **name them as fast as you can***.*

● *Let's practise first with the pictures below. They show a rabbit, a cat, a horse, a fish and a butterfly. Can you name them, as fast as you can, in the order that you see them?*

● *Now let's do two more sheets of them.*

● *Try this one first* (give the child Picture sheet 1).

● *Are you ready? Start . . .* (start the timer).

Record the time taken on the Marking sheet.

● *Now let's do the same for the second one. Remember to go as fast as you can* (give him/her Picture sheet 2).

Record the time taken on the Marking sheet.

Errors are not penalised. Usually a child notices a mistake, and corrects it; but do *not* deduct points for mistakes that are not corrected.

Photocopy master published by Hodder Education

Picture Naming – Picture sheet 1

Picture Naming – Picture sheet 2

Picture Naming – Marking sheet

Pupil's Name: _____

Date of assessment: _____

Picture Sheet 1 = ☐ seconds

Picture Sheet 2 = ☐ seconds

Total time taken (1 + 2) = ☐ seconds

Backward Span – Instructions

Equipment required

● Marking sheet   ● Pencil

Instructions to be read out to the child

● *I'm going to say some words. Then I want you to say them* ***backwards***.

● *I'll show you what I mean:*
if I say: 'bus, book', you say 'book, bus';
or if I say: 'apple, piano, football', you say 'football, piano, apple'.

● *Now you try. I'll say some words, then you say them backwards . . .*

Continue until the child makes mistakes in three consecutive questions.

Discuss any errors with the child, letting them know what the correct answer would have been.

Tell the child each time there is an increase in the number of words to remember
(e.g. from two to three words in the sequence).

Tips

• Score as 1 only if *exactly* correct. Otherwise give a score of 0.

• Read out the words at a moderate pace. Reading at too fast or too slow a pace can increase the difficulty of this task.

• Break for a couple of seconds between each question to allow the child to regain concentration.

• Do not repeat any of the questions.

Photocopy master published by Hodder Education

Backward Span – Marking sheet

Pupil's Name: _____

Date of assessment: _____

Score each question as 1 = all correct or 0 = incorrect.

No.								Score
1	cat	four						
2	lorry	coat						
3	fork	zebra						
4	mug	snake	ring					
5	ten	white	window					
6	door	ferry	red					
7	jet	horse	dress	blue				
8	twelve	walk	navy	butterfly				
9	two	skis	purse	bowl				
10	shoe	cow	eight	van	table			
11	pan	green	taxi	pink	one			
12	spoon	orange	tie	three	boat			
13	cooker	shirt	gerbil	thirteen	black	plane		
14	car	chair	giraffe	six	brown	fourteen		
15	bird	nine	trousers	yellow	five	skates		
16	eleven	plate	glasses	pig	seven	sock	cream	
17	mouse	cup	purple	hat	dog	glove	bicycle	
18	dish	grey	scarf	rabbit	carpet	watch	scooter	

Total score [ ]

Photocopy master published by Hodder Education

Visual Memory – Instructions

Equipment required

- Flashcards
- Marking sheet
- 'Window' Viewer
- Pencil
- Examples sheet
- Answer sheet

Instructions to be read out to the child

- *I am going to show you some cards with some shapes on them.*
  You'll only be shown each card for a very short time, just a few seconds.
  You have to try to remember what shape or shapes you have seen.

- *Let's try two for practice, to show you what I mean.*

Show the child the Example 1 flashcard for **3 seconds**, before placing it out of sight. Then give the child the Examples sheet, with the window viewer showing the first line of shapes. Explain that they have to look in the 'window' each time and tick the shape(s) they have seen. Discuss how the window will be moved down to show a new line of shapes after each card is shown.

N.B. that it is crucial that the **window is not moved down until the flashcard is out of sight!**

Repeat for Example 2, then give the child the Answer sheet proper.

- *OK, now let's try the rest of them . . .*

Tips

- Cut out the Window Viewer and prepare the Flashcards first.

- Be consistent with the length of time you show each flashcard: 3 seconds only for each card.

- Do not re-show any card.

- Score as 1 only if all shapes on that flashcard are remembered correctly. Otherwise, score as 0.

- Do not include the score for the two example cards in the overall score.

- The Marking sheet shows only the correct shapes: photocopy on to acetate for ease of marking.

Photocopy master published by Hodder Education

Example 1   ▯ ▣ ╱

_____

Example 2   ⌐ + ⋈ ⩑

_____

Photocopy master published by Hodder Education

Visual Memory – Answer sheet

Pupil's Name: _____

Date of assessment: _____

Card 1 _____ 1/0

Card 2 _____ 1/0

Card 3 _____ 1/0

Card 4 _____ 1/0

Card 5 _____ 1/0

Card 6 _____ 1/0

Card 7 _____ 1/0

Card 8 _____ 1/0

Card 9 _____ 1/0

Card 10 _____ 1/0

Card 11 _____ 1/0

Card 12 _____ 1/0

Total score ☐

Photocopy master published by Hodder Education

CUT OUT SHADED AREA

Photocopy master published by Hodder Education

Visual Memory – Flashcards

- Ideally, photocopy these pages on to card, cut each card to approximately A5 size, and keep them for future re-use.

- There are fourteen flashcards altogether: two examples and twelve 'test' cards.

- Familiarise yourself with the cards before using them.

- Practise showing them for just 3 seconds.

Photocopy master published by Hodder Education

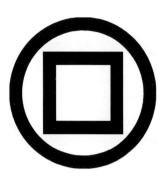

Example 1

✂ ....

Visual Memory

Example 2

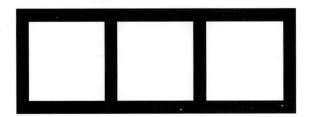

Card 1

Visual Memory

Card 2

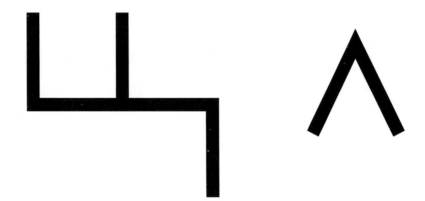

Card 3

Visual Memory

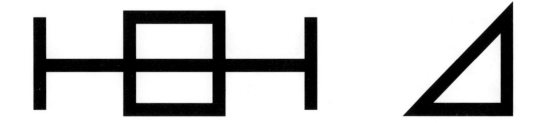

Card 4

Visual Memory

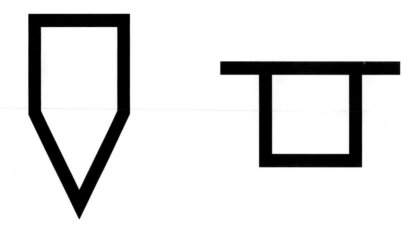

Card 5

✂ ....

Visual Memory

Card 6

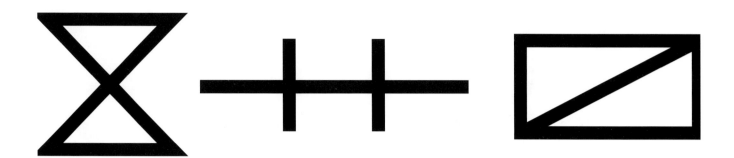

Card 7

Card 8

Visual Memory

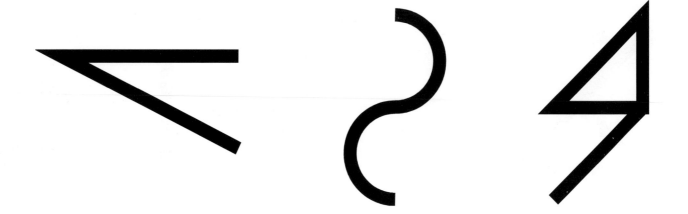

Card 9

Visual Memory

Card 10

Card 11

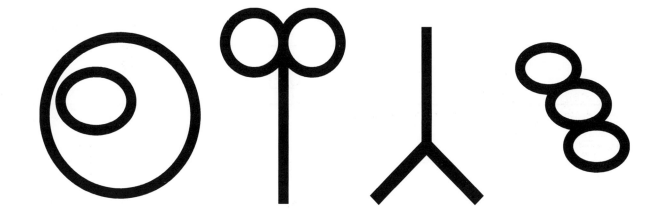

Card 12

Visual Memory – Marking sheet

Card 1 _____

Card 2 _____

Card 3 _____

Card 4 _____

Card 5 _____

Card 6 _____

Card 7 _____

Card 8 _____

Card 9 _____

Card 10 _____

Card 11 _____

Card 12 _____

Vergence & Visual Tracking – Instructions

Equipment required

- Marking sheet
- 2 pens/pencils

Instructions to be read out to the child

Task 1

- *In this task, I am going to watch how your eyes move as they follow a moving point.*

- *Follow the top of this pencil as I move it from side to side.*
  You have to keep your head completely still, only moving your eyes to follow it.

- *Try not to take your eyes off the top at any time!*

Move the pencil slowly from side to side about an arm's length away from the child.
Repeat until you can clearly describe how his/her eyes move.

- *Now, do the same again as I move it around in circles.*

Move the pencil around in a clockwise then anti-clockwise direction.

Once clear what happens, record this on the Marking sheet by **ticking one of the Task 1 boxes**.

Task 2

- *Now, I want **you** to hold the pencil in one hand, with your arm out straight.*
  Now, whilst looking at the top of the pencil, bring it in slowly to touch your nose.

(You may wish to demonstrate this to the child.)

Record how the child's eyes converge as they follow the pencil (i.e. is a good squint achieved?).
Record this by ticking one of the Task 2 boxes.

Task 3

- *Finally, I want you to do an exercise using two pencils.*

Get the child to hold one of the pencils approximately 8 inches (20cm) in front of their nose, with the other pencil being held level to this, but approximately 8 inches (20cm) to the right.

- *OK, what I want you to do is to look from the top of one pencil to the top of the other, then back again to the first pencil. Do this as quickly as you can. Keep doing it till I tell you to stop.*

You are interested in whether there is a saccadic lag – i.e. is there an unexpected delay when trying to move his/her fixation from one pencil to the other? **Record this by ticking one of the Task 3 boxes.**

Vergence & Visual Tracking – Marking sheet

Pupil's Name: _____

Date of assessment: _____

Tick three boxes in total.

Only tick one for each task.

No apparent difficulties	Possible area of difficulty
• **Task 1** The eyes move smoothly from side to side, and in circles, with no flicker or irregularity. ☐ *Score 0*	• **Task 1** Tracking is not completely smooth. Instead, at times, the eyes may flicker or jump. ☐ *Score 1*
• **Task 2** The eyes converge effectively as the pencil is moved in towards the nose. A clear squint is achieved. ☐ *Score 0*	• **Task 2** The eyes will begin to converge effectively. However, this will stop prematurely with one or both eyes suddenly diverging outwards. ☐ *Score 1*
• **Task 3** The eyes move quickly and easily as they look from one pencil to the other. ☐ *Score 0*	• **Task 3** There is an unexpected time delay as the eyes try to look from one pencil to the other. ☐ *Score 1*

Total score ☐

Figure Copying – Instructions

Equipment required

- Examples sheet
- Answer sheet
- Marking guide
- Pencil

Instructions to be read out to the child

- *I'm going to give you some shapes to copy. You have to copy them as best you can.*

- *Let's look at an example first to show you what I mean.*

Talk through the example given (use the Examples sheet).

- *Now you have to do some. Here they are on a sheet for you. Start when you are ready. There is no time limit for doing this.*

Tip

It is strongly recommended that you photocopy the Marking guide on to acetate, so it can be placed over the Answer sheet to compare the child's own drawings directly with those of the Marking guide.

Photocopy master published by Hodder Education

Figure Copying – Examples

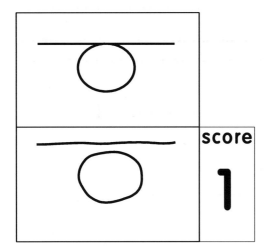

Quite good, but line too high.

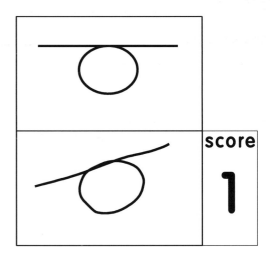

Quite good, but line at wrong angle.

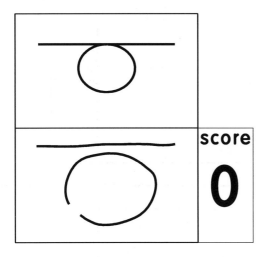

Not good, circle too large, incomplete and does not touch the line.

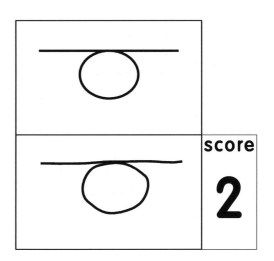

Very good.

Figure Copying – Answer sheet

Pupil's Name: _____

Date of assessment: _____

1 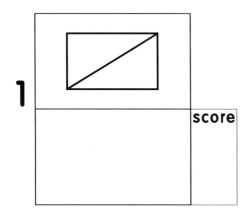 score

2 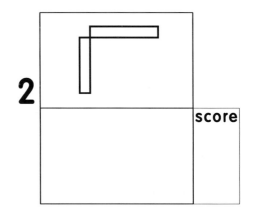 score

3 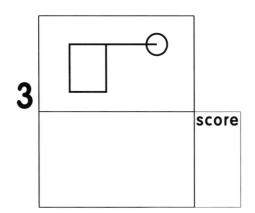 score

4 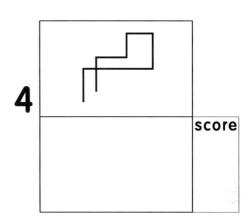 score

5 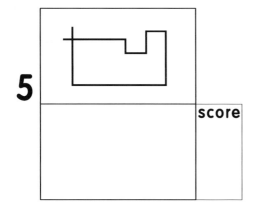 score

6 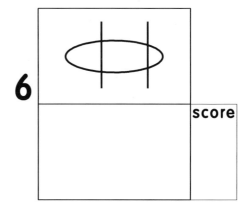 score

Total score

Figure Copying – Marking guide

- There are a possible 3 marks for each drawing: 18 in total.
- If a drawing deviates significantly from the target figure, score zero.
- Otherwise, mark separately for the accuracy of size, angles and how the lines are joined.
- Place this Marking guide over the Answer sheet and compare each drawing in turn:

A: Overall size (within 20%) – Compare with figure A, below: the size of the child's drawing should be between the two figures shown **[1 mark]**.

B: Angles drawn (within 10°) – Compare with figure B, below: the angles in the child's drawing should be no greater/lesser than those shown **[1 mark]**.

C: Lines joined accurately (within 5–10%) – Compare with figure C: the lines in the child's drawing should be joined at least as well as those shown **[1 mark]**.

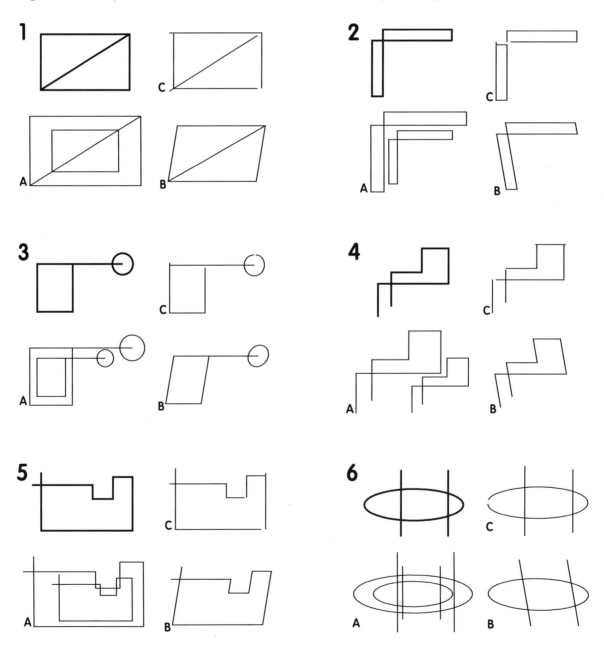

Balancing Task – Instructions

Equipment required

- Balancing marking sheet
- Pencil
- Book or books to stand on: choose a sturdy

book or books that are longer than the length of the child's foot and *together* are between 4cm and 10cm thick.

This task requires the child to keep balanced while carrying out a cognitive task. The child has to balance on the books on one leg, first with both eyes open, then with both eyes closed, while doing the tasks you have chosen.

For safety reasons, carry out this task in an open space away from any furniture or sharp edges, etc, which may cause the child injury if he/she were to overbalance. The book/s must not be more than 10cm high.

Here are the tasks – choose ones that she/ he should find quite difficult, but still be reasonably successful at:

Common sequences

- Recite the days of the week
- Recite them backwards
- Recite the months of the year
- Recite them backwards

Counting Backwards

- Count backwards from five
- Count backwards from ten
- Count backwards from ten in steps of two
- Count backwards from twenty in steps of three

Instructions to be read out to the child

- I am going to give you some things to do, and you are going to try to do them **whilst balancing on one leg.**
- I need you to stand on top of this book/s, on one leg. You have got to try your best to stay balancing at all times!

(If right-footed, get him/her to balance on the left-leg. If left-footed, get him/her to balance on the right leg. If unsure which is their dominant foot, get them to kick a ball to see.)

Select four tasks – two Common Sequences and two Counting Backwards.

Ask him/her to do **one of the Common Sequences and one of the Counting Backwards questions whilst balancing with <u>both eyes open</u>.**

Then ask him/her to do the **remaining two questions whilst balancing, but this time with <u>both eyes closed</u>.**

Use the Marking Sheet to record what happens, and use the graph at the end to decide to decide whether there are no apparent difficulties (score above the 50% line), some difficulties (score between the 25 and 50%) or obvious difficulties (below the 25% line).

N.B. *This task is often difficult to score. Do not stick rigidly to the balancing scale provided, but use your own judgement about the degree of difficulty shown. Your focus is solely the child's ability to balance, **not** the accuracy of the answers.*

Balancing Task – Marking sheet

Pupil's Name: _____

Date of assessment: _____

Tick only <u>one</u> box in each column. In each case, form an overall judgement based on the child's performance on both tasks.

Eyes open   **Eyes closed**

Eyes open	Eyes closed	
0 ☐	0 ☐	No movement.
1 ☐	1 ☐	Slight movement of arms and/or legs to retain balance.
2 ☐	2 ☐	Significant movement of arms and/or legs to retain balance.
3 ☐	3 ☐	Occasional balance loss. However, by placing his/her other foot on the ground avoids falling off the book/s.
4 ☐	4 ☐	Frequent balance loss, but by placing his/her other foot on the ground avoids falling off the book/s. (But if this is <u>very</u> frequent, then score as 6 – enormous difficulty balancing.)

0

1

2

3 & 4

Total score (eyes open + eyes closed) ☐

Photocopy master published by Hodder Education

Bilateral Integration – Instructions

Equipment required

● Large pair of scissors   ● Answer sheet   ● Marking guide   ● Pencil

Instructions to be read out to the child

Place a large pair of scissors in front of the child, open as if ready to cut, with the handles towards the child.

● *I want you to draw these scissors on this sheet of paper. Don't worry if you are not very good at drawing, because that is not what I am interested in.*

● *There is no time limit for this. Start when you are ready.*

Use the Marking guide to score the drawing.

Bilateral Integration – Answer sheet

Pupil's Name: _____

Date of assessment: _____

Draw the pair of scissors in the space below:

Bilateral Integration – Marking guide

Do not score the quality of the drawing – you are concerned with the cross-over:

- Do the two pieces cross over at all? If not, there is a serious difficulty. *Score as 'very poorly developed'.*

- Do they cross, but in a way that is inaccurate or wrongly positioned? *Score as 'a little weak'.*

- They are crossed correctly, and are in proportion. *Score as 'no apparent problems'.*

For example:

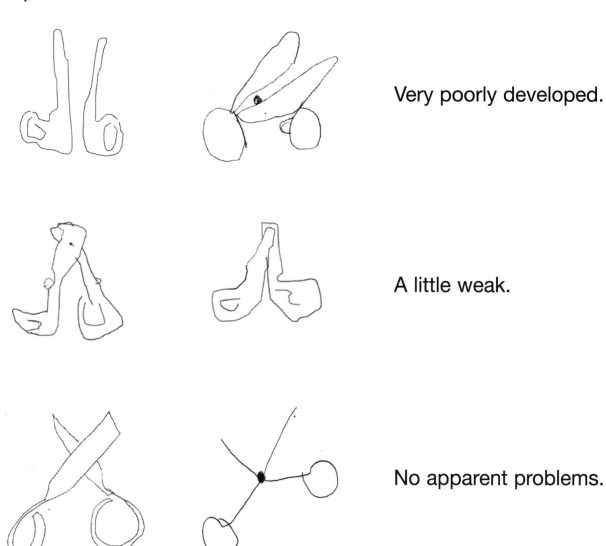

Very poorly developed.

A little weak.

No apparent problems.

Photocopy master published by Hodder Education

Interpretation graph: Picture Naming

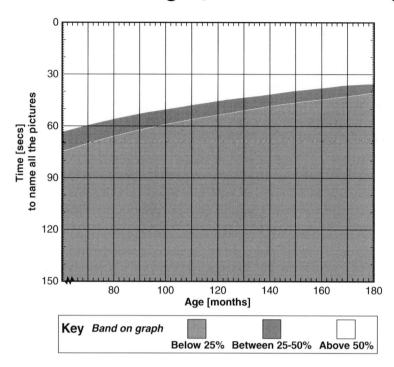

Interpretation graph: Backward Span

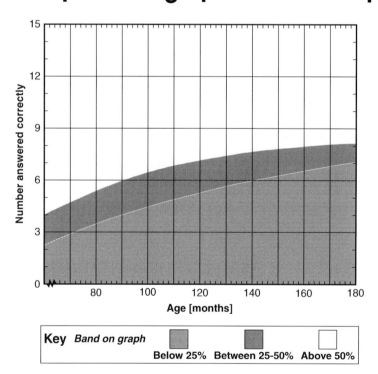

Interpretation graph: Visual Memory

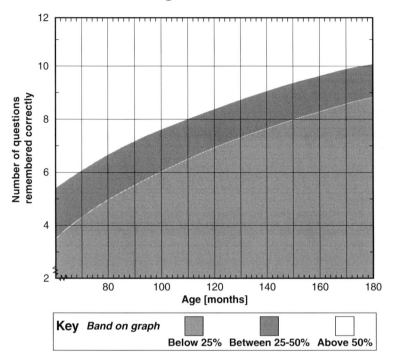

Interpretation graph: Figure Copying

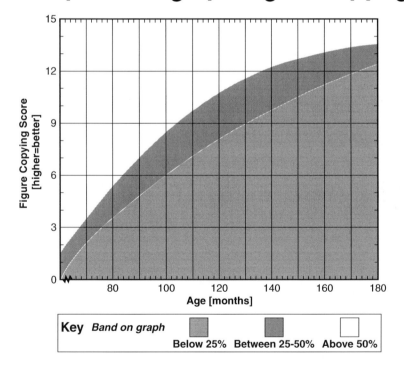

Interpretation graph: Balancing

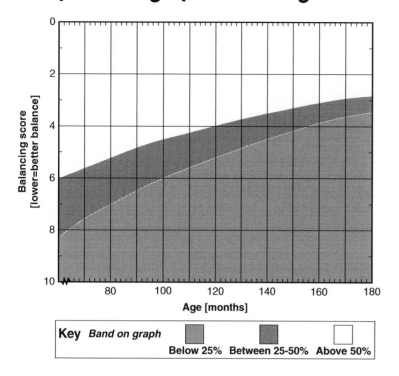